Gennaro's
FAST COOK ITALIAN

First published in 2018 by

INTERLINK BOOKS

An imprint of Interlink Publishing Group, Inc.

46 Crosby Street, Northampton, MA 01060

www.interlinkbooks.com

Copyright © Pavilion Books Company Ltd 2018

Text copyright © Gennaro Contaldo 2018

American edition copyright © Interlink Publishing Group, Inc. 2018

All rights reserved. No part of this publication may be reproduced,
stored in a retrieval system, or transmitted in any form or by any means
electronic, mechanical, photocopying, recording or otherwise, without
the prior written permission of the copyright owner.

Library of Congress Cataloging-in-Publication Data available

ISBN 978-1-62371-980-7

10 9 8 7 6 5 4 3 2 1

Reproduction by Mission, Hong Kong

Printed and bound by 1010 Printing International Ltd, China

To request our 48-page, full-color catalog, please call us toll free at
1-800-238-LINK, visit our website at www.interlinkbooks.com, or send
us an e-mail at: info@interlinkbooks.com.

Gennaro's
FAST COOK ITALIAN

Gennaro Contaldo

Interlink Books

An imprint of Interlink Publishing Group, Inc.
Northampton, Massachusetts

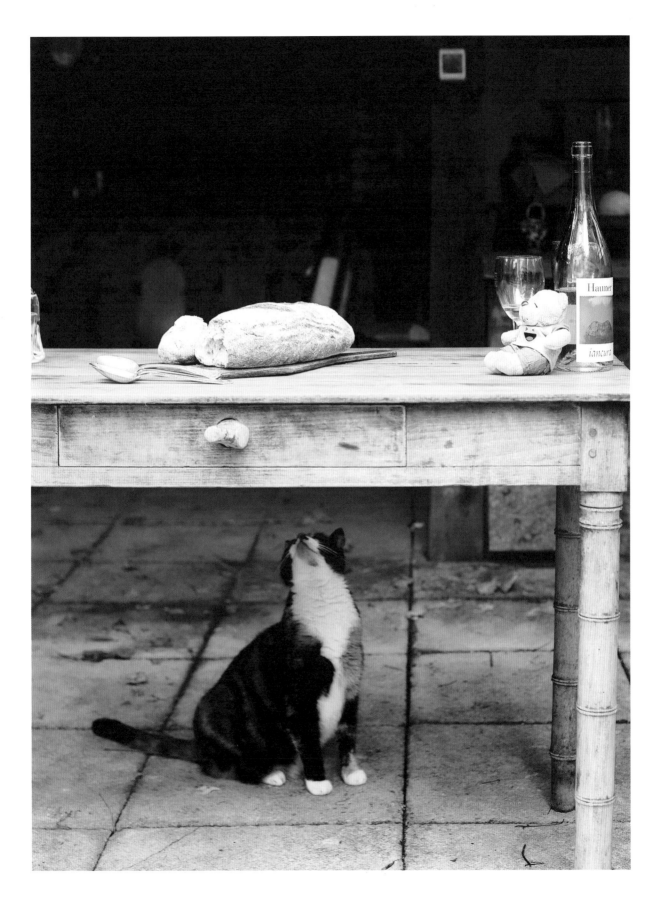

CONTENTS

ITALIAN FAST COOKING

Fast cooking doesn't have to mean unhealthy fast food. In fact, quite the opposite! The Italian philosophy of using a few good ingredients and cooking them in a simple, unfussy way means you can create beautiful, nutritious dishes in no time. Traditionally, some of the best Italian dishes are made quickly with just a few fresh or stored ingredients.

These days, not all Italians have the time to cook lengthy meals like they used to—gone are the days when women stayed at home and made pasta by hand, or soaked beans in preparation for a slow-cooked pot of soup or stew. Don't get me wrong, I, like most Italians, still love to cook like this, but perhaps on weekends or for festivities like Christmas and Easter, when I have more time to cook. During a normal week, when the family is at work and school, there just isn't the time to prepare the dishes that our grandmothers once made.

Italians mainly cook from scratch and use high-quality, seasonal ingredients. This doesn't mean starting to cook the night before, but a little planning in advance to ensure you have the right ingredients in your pantry is a good start. Take pasta or risotto, for example; these two classic staples of Italian cooking, so quick and simple to prepare, make excellent, nutritious meals that everyone can enjoy at any time. I always make sure I have a selection of dried pasta in the pantry, as well as risotto rice, good olive oil, stock, and cans of tomatoes. Add some onions, carrots, garlic, pancetta, and Parmesan from the fridge and I can already see quite a few meals. Even when the cabinets are bare, a quick dish of *spaghetti aglio, olio e peperoncino* (spaghetti with garlic, oil, and chili) is a popular standby, especially among Italian youngsters who opt for it as a midnight snack after a night on the town!

Of course, Italian food is not just pasta, and there are so many meat, fish, and vegetable dishes that can be prepared in little time. Fish, chicken, thin slices of meat, as well as eggs for delicious omelets cook in no time and provide nourishing meals. Vegetables are also often used in the Italian kitchen to create delicious main dishes that cook quickly. Italian cooking doesn't need too many added flavors, sauces, or marinades, since Italians prefer to buy fresh, quality ingredients, which speak for themselves! Take a simple steak, for example—as long as you buy the best piece of meat you can afford, just a little salt and pepper and some oil are all that you really need; while the steak

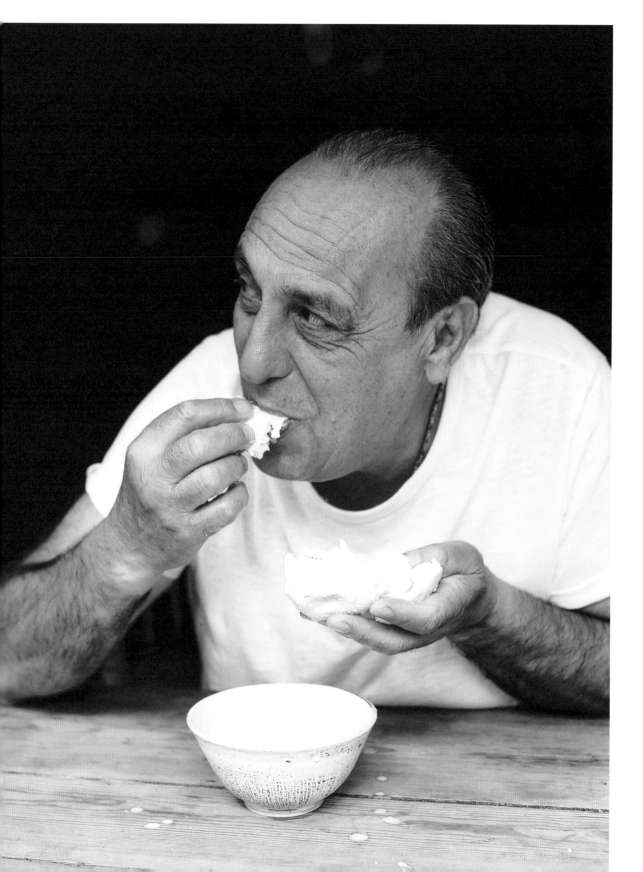

is grilling, broiling, or frying, slice some tomatoes and red onions for a side salad. Serve it with some good bread and you have a delicious meal fit for a king, which has taken far less time to prepare than waiting for takeout to arrive! And, of course, it is far more nutritious and enjoyable to eat!

To make life even simpler, there are all kinds of short cuts available these days; walk into any supermarket and you will find a wide variety of ready-chopped and spiralized vegetables, as well as cubed pancetta, grated cheeses, and canned beans and legumes. Italian delis stock good-quality fresh sauces like pesto, tomato sauce, and many others, as well as mouth-watering pickled vegetables in jars, which are always handy to keep in your pantry. You can of course make your own sauces; it's always a good idea to make a large quantity of say tomato sauce perhaps once a month (time-permitting) and freeze in batches to use whenever required. On a weekly basis, if you have time, you could chop or grate a few basic vegetables, like onions, carrots, celery, zucchini, garlic, and so on, store them in containers in the fridge, and use them in your cooking throughout the week. You could also grate a quantity of Parmesan cheese and chop pieces of pancetta so you have these on hand, too. This way, you know you will be using the freshest ingredients for all your dishes as well as reducing so much of your preparation time when it comes to cooking. In fact, a little planning ahead at the beginning of the week will make cooking easier, stress free, and will ensure healthy balanced meals at all times with minimum fuss and effort.

Overleaf, you will find my list of essentials for your pantry and fridge, which will give you more than enough for quick and simple meals at any time. Obviously, add some meat and fish to this and your meal planning will be taken care of.

All the recipes in this book have been carefully chosen to ensure they are quick and effortless to prepare and cook. They are all super simple to follow and even someone with only basic cooking skills will be able to make them. Although perfect for everyday cooking, most of the recipes can also be made for special occasions—why spend hours in the kitchen just because you have guests coming or you are making a celebratory meal?

I hope you enjoy cooking the recipes in this book, which I hope will prove invaluable not just for when you are looking for a quick dish to rustle up, but for all your daily meals—simple recipes for life that can be used over and over again.

Enjoy, happy cooking, and *buon appetito*!

GENNARO

MY ITALIAN KITCHEN ESSENTIALS

I have put together a basic list of essential Italian ingredients that I believe will help you in your meal planning. Keep an eye on your supplies and, when something runs out, make sure it is replaced.

PANTRY

Extra-virgin olive oil, for dressing
Olive oil or vegetable oil, for frying
Anchovies
Capers
Dried porcini
Green and black olives
Dried oregano
Dried hot red pepper flakes
Natural breadcrumbs
Chopped walnuts
Sea salt and black pepper
Jars of good-quality preserved vegetables—
    eggplants, zucchini, bell peppers, artichokes, sun-
    dried tomatoes
Dried pasta—a selection of long and short varieties
Vegetable stock—I also like to keep chicken, beef,
    and fish stock, but as long as you have a supply of
    vegetable stock, you can make most dishes
Red or white wine vinegar
Wine—red and white
Pesto
All-purpose flour
Risotto rice (such as Arborio) and long-grain rice
Quick-cooking polenta cornmeal
Cans of beans and legumes—cannellini, borlotti
    (cranberry), chickpeas, lentils
Cans of chopped tomatoes, and tomato passata
    (strained tomato purée) or tomato purée
Grissini breadsticks
Pane carasau (wafer-thin Sardinian flatbread)

REFRIGERATOR

Parmesan
Ricotta
Mascarpone
Mozzarella—bufala to enjoy fresh in salads or
    appetizers, and a harder variety for cooking with
Pancetta or bacon
Prosciutto—this usually has a good sell-by date and is
    handy to keep for a quick antipasto or snack
Organic free-range eggs
Good-quality gnocchi from a deli

FREEZER

Peas
Fava beans
Berries
Homemade tomato sauce (see p.185)

FRESH PRODUCE

Onions—white and red
Garlic
Red chili pepper
Carrots
Celery
Zucchini
Potatoes
Salad—romaine, little gem lettuce, and salad greens
Tomatoes
Selection of bell peppers
Herbs—parsley, rosemary, sage, thyme, mint

SALADS

Salads have come a long way from the days of unappetizing, limp lettuce leaves and tasteless tomatoes. Salad dressings have evolved too, and now interesting ingredients are put together to make delicious salads that don't necessarily have to be eaten as a side dish, but can also be enjoyed as a main course.

Italians love salads and most meals include a salad of some sort—it could be chargrilled bell peppers with garlic and olive oil, or thinly sliced zucchini with white wine vinegar and fresh mint, or simply a mix of seasonal green leaves. *Prosciutto crudo* is probably one of Italy's most loved and well-known ingredients. Although here it is known simply as "prosciutto," in Italy prosciutto means "ham," which can be either *cotto* (cooked) or *crudo* (raw or cured). It marries very well with fruit—melon is probably the one that always springs to mind; I must admit this is one of my favorite combinations, especially during the summer when cantaloupe is at its most refreshing (see the recipe on p.32). Figs are also a firm favorite and so are peaches, again, during the summer months, when they are at their best. Autumnal fruits such as plums, apples, and pears all make delicious combinations.

Dressings in Italy tend to be delicate and uncomplicated, and the classic olive oil and vinegar, or olive oil and lemon juice, are still my favorites. Always use good-quality extra-virgin olive oil and wine vinegar, and dress your salads just before serving to avoid soggy leaves. I tend to sprinkle a little salt over my salads first, before adding two parts olive oil to one part vinegar or lemon juice.

Most of the salads in this book are also suitable to enjoy as appetizers, or to serve at parties or as accompaniments to a barbecue. They are a light and enjoyable way to pack in your "five a day," so, whether you serve them as an accompaniment or as a main course, you can be sure you are eating a healthy, nutritious dish.

INSALATA DI GAMBERI E ASPARAGI

SHRIMP AND ASPARAGUS SALAD

A quick and healthy salad, which can be eaten as a light lunch or served as an antipasto with some good bread.

Cooking time: 12–15 minutes

Serves 4

9 oz/250 g asparagus tips
2 tbsp extra-virgin olive oil
1 garlic clove, finely chopped
1 tbsp finely chopped parsley
10½ oz/300 g raw jumbo shrimp
juice and peeled zest of 1 lemon,
   zest finely chopped
1½ tbsp/¾ oz/20 g butter
sea salt and freshly ground black pepper

Bring a saucepan of water to a boil, add the asparagus tips, and simmer for about 3 minutes, until just tender. Drain and set aside.

Meanwhile, in a frying pan set over medium heat, heat the olive oil, add the garlic and parsley, and sweat for 1 minute. Add the shrimp and fry, stirring, for a couple of minutes, until cooked. Stir in the chopped lemon zest and juice, remove from the heat, and set aside.

In another frying pan, melt the butter, add the cooked asparagus, season with some salt and pepper, and fry, stirring, for 1 minute. Remove from the heat, then arrange on a serving dish, together with the cooked shrimp, pouring over the pan juices.

INSALATA DI FAGIOLINI

GREEN BEAN SALAD

This lovely, crunchy salad can be eaten warm or cold, and so can be made in advance, if desired. It makes a lovely accompaniment to grilled meat or fish, or frittata. If you prefer a milder dressing, then simply reduce the amount of mustard. To save time, buy pre-trimmed green beans.

Cooking time: 10 minutes

Serves 2–4

6¼ oz/180 g green beans, trimmed
5¾ oz/160 g sugar snap peas
½ red onion, or 1 banana shallot

For the dressing:
1 small garlic clove
2 tbsp extra-virgin olive oil
1 tbsp red wine vinegar
1 tsp mustard
sea salt

Place the green beans in a large saucepan, cover with water, and bring to a boil. Reduce the heat and simmer for about 6 minutes, then add the sugar snaps and continue to cook for a couple of minutes, until tender. Make sure not to overcook the vegetables. Drain and set aside.

Meanwhile, finely slice the onion or shallot and set aside.

Make the dressing. Finely chop the garlic and combine with the olive oil, vinegar, mustard, and a little salt, to taste.

Place the drained vegetables in a serving bowl, add the onion or shallot, and pour over the dressing before serving.

INSALATA DI PATATE
WARM POTATO SALAD WITH RED ONION AND MINT

In Italy, when Italians make potato salad, they usually flavor it with dried oregano. Here, to give the salad a fresh summery flavor, I have added fresh mint. Marinating the onions while waiting for the potatoes to cook gives a nice vinegary kick to the dish and, unless you really like lots of vinegar, you don't need to add any more to the salad. However, don't get rid of the vinegar marinade, because you can use it again. You could also marinate more onions than you need, keep them in the refrigerator, and use them to liven up other salads or sandwiches.

Cooking time: 12 minutes

Serves 4

14 oz/400 g baby potatoes, washed,
   skins kept on
1 small red onion
sea salt and freshly ground black pepper
⅔ cup/150 ml white wine vinegar
3 tbsp extra-virgin olive oil
12 mint leaves, coarsely chopped, to serve

Boil the potatoes in a large saucepan for about 10 minutes, until tender.

Meanwhile, finely slice the onion and place it in a small bowl with a pinch of salt. Cover with the vinegar.

Drain the potatoes and transfer to a serving bowl. Drain the marinated onions and add them to the potatoes, mixing gently. Drizzle with olive oil, season with salt and pepper, and scatter with chopped mint leaves before serving.

INSALATA DI FAVE E CARCIOFI

FAVA BEAN AND ARTICHOKE SALAD WITH ARUGULA AND PARMESAN

A quick and simple salad using preserved artichokes, which are available in good Italian delis, and convenient frozen fava beans, which are lightly cooked until tender. It can be served as an appetizer, as a side to lamb dishes (see Anchovy-Infused Lamb Cutlets, p.122), or as a light lunch with some crusty bread.

Cooking time: 10 minutes

Serves 2–4

⅔ cup/3½ oz/100 g frozen shelled fava beans
2½ tbsp/¾ oz/20 g pine nuts
5½ oz/150 g artichoke hearts preserved in oil,
    drained
2 handfuls of arugula
⅓ cup/1 oz/30 g shaved Parmesan

For the dressing:
2 tbsp extra-virgin olive oil
juice of ½ lemon
sea salt

Bring a small saucepan of water to a boil over medium heat, add the fava beans, bring back to a boil, and cook for 3 minutes.

Meanwhile, heat a small frying pan over medium heat and toast the pine nuts for about 3 minutes. Remove from the heat and set aside to cool.

Drain the cooked fava beans in a colander, then rinse them under cold running water to cool them down; drain well. Remove the outer skins and place the beans in a bowl, together with the artichokes, arugula, cooled pine nuts, and Parmesan shavings.

Combine the dressing ingredients, pour over the salad, mix well, and serve.

CARPACCIO DI ZUCCHINI
ZUCCHINI CARPACCIO WITH PECORINO, MINT, AND POMEGRANATE

Zucchini is so versatile and, when used raw, makes a lovely appetizer or side salad. Make sure you use very fresh zucchini and slice them as thinly as you can. Ready-to-use pomegranate seeds are widely available in supermarkets all year round and not only look great, but also make a nutritious addition to this simple, delicious dish.

Preparation time: 15 minutes

Serves 4

2 zucchini
¼ cup/60 ml extra-virgin olive oil
2 tbsp white wine vinegar
1 garlic clove, very finely chopped
1 tbsp finely chopped fresh mint, plus a few
    extra leaves, to garnish
sea salt
⅓ cup/1¾ oz/50 g pomegranate seeds
⅓ cup/1 oz/30 g shaved Pecorino

Using a vegetable peeler or a mandolin, slice thin slivers of zucchini lengthways and set aside.

In a bowl, combine the olive oil, white wine vinegar, garlic, chopped mint, and salt to taste, and whisk for a minute or so, until the mixture thickens slightly.

Dip the zucchini slices in the dressing, then arrange them on a serving plate. Pour over the remaining dressing, scatter with the pomegranate seeds and Pecorino shavings, then garnish with the extra mint leaves and serve.

INSALATA DI RISO VENERE

BLACK RICE SALAD

This unusual nutritious rice, with its highly beneficial health properties, is becoming increasingly popular in Italy, appearing on restaurant menus and on supermarket shelves. Originating in China, black rice was favored by ancient emperors for its nutritional and aphrodisiacal properties, hence the name *venere* (deriving from Venus). It is now cultivated in the rice fields of northern Italy. It is a perfect rice for salads and makes a delicious, healthy lunch or, if made in a larger quantity, is ideal to serve at parties.

Cooking time: 20–25 minutes

Serves 4

1½ cups/10½ oz/300 g black rice (*riso venere*)
½ red bell pepper, finely chopped
½ yellow bell pepper, finely chopped
2 avocados, finely chopped
6 cherry tomatoes, quartered
7 oz/200 g mozzarella or feta, cut into
    small cubes
about 12 chives, finely chopped
⅓ cup/1¾ oz/50 g pomegranate seeds
⅓ cup/80 ml extra-virgin olive oil
juice of 1 lemon
sea salt

Place the rice in a saucepan with double its volume of cold water (about 3 cups/700 ml). Place over medium heat, bring to a boil, then turn the heat down and gently simmer for 15–17 minutes, until *al dente*.

Drain the rice, rinse under cold running water to cool, then drain well again. Place in a serving bowl, together with the vegetables, mozzarella, chives, and pomegranate seeds. Drizzle with the olive oil and lemon juice, add salt to taste, and mix together well.

INSALATA DI CECI

CHICKPEA SALAD WITH OLIVES, AMALFI LEMON, AND MINT

This simple, fresh salad can be served as part of an antipasto or eaten as a main course with some bread. If made in a large quantity, it is perfect to serve at parties. Choose good-quality olives and if you can't find Amalfi lemons, buy the best you can afford for maximum taste.

Preparation time: 10 minutes

Serves 2–4

1 large Amalfi lemon
1 × 14-oz/400-g can of chickpeas, drained
¼ rosemary sprig
¼ thyme sprig
2 cups/7 oz/200 g mixed green and black
    pitted olives (Kalamata and Gaeta types,
    if possible)
a small handful of fresh mint leaves,
    roughly torn
¼ fresh red chili pepper, finely chopped
2 tbsp extra-virgin olive oil
sea salt

Slice the lemon in half. Sqeeze the juice of one half and set it aside. Thinly slice the other lemon half, and cut each slice into quarters.

In a serving bowl, combine the drained chickpeas, rosemary, thyme, whole olives, lemon slices, mint, and chili pepper. Drizzle with the olive oil and lemon juice and add some salt, to taste. Mix together well and serve.

INSALATA DI PISELLI FRESCHI E BURRATA

FRESH PEA AND BURRATA SALAD WITH SUNFLOWER-SEED CROSTINI

This is a lovely salad to make during the spring, when fresh peas are available. For speed, you can buy ready-shelled peas. Burrata is a fresh cheese from Puglia that looks like mozzarella but has a very creamy interior. Italian delis and good supermarkets will stock it, but if you prefer, you can use *bufala* (buffalo) mozzarella instead. This dish makes a fantastic appetizer or can be enjoyed as a delicious, light lunch, accompanied by the crostini.

Cooking time: 15 minutes

Serves 4

1¼ cups/6 oz/175 g fresh podded peas
generous 2 cups/3 oz/90 g watercress
Leaves of 1–2 romaine lettuce hearts
9 oz/250 g burrata or buffalo mozzarella

For the crostini:
⅓ cup/1¾ oz/50 g sunflower seeds
a handful of fresh basil leaves
1 tbsp extra-virgin olive oil
a pinch of sea salt
a pinch of red pepper flakes
4 slices of good-quality crusty wholewheat
    bread with seeds, toasted

For the dressing:
2 tbsp extra-virgin olive oil
1 tbsp lemon juice
sea salt and freshly ground black pepper

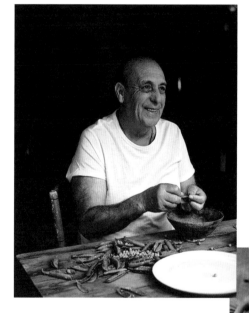

Bring a saucepan of water to a boil, add the peas, and cook for about 2 minutes, until tender but not overcooked. Drain, rinse under cold running water, and drain well.

Meanwhile, prepare the crostini. Place the sunflower seeds, basil leaves, and olive oil in a blender or food processor and process until you obtain a smooth consistency. Combine with the salt and red pepper flakes. Toast the bread and spread with the sunflower seed paste. Set aside.

Combine the dressing ingredients.

Arrange the watercress and lettuce leaves on a large serving plate, sprinkle on the cooked peas, and pour over half of the dressing. Gently break up the burrata or mozzarella and scatter over the greens. Drizzle with the remaining dressing and serve with the crostini on the side.

INSALATA DI POMODORI MISTI

OREGANO-INFUSED MIXED TOMATO SALAD

A tomato salad, such as this one, was often served during the summer when I was a child growing up in southern Italy. Tomatoes were nearly always served with local, dried oregano and fresh basil. Simply dressed, with good extra-virgin olive oil and salt, I could easily eat this every day during the summer, served with some *fresella* (double-baked bread). *Cipollotti* or spring onions are large scallions and can sometimes be found in markets. Alternatively, substitute with some chopped scallions.

Preparation time: 5 minutes

Serves 2–4

1 lb 2 oz/500 g good-quality mixed tomatoes
   (red, yellow, orange)
1 *cipollotto* (spring onion), or 2 large scallions,
   finely sliced
1 garlic clove, very finely chopped
a pinch of dried oregano
½ handful of basil leaves
3 tbsp extra-virgin olive oil
sea salt

Slice the tomatoes and arrange them on a serving dish or in a bowl. Scatter with the sliced onion, garlic, oregano, and basil. Drizzle with olive oil, add salt to taste, then mix well and serve.

INSALATA DI LENTICCHIE

LENTIL SALAD

You could make this with pre-cooked canned lentils, but I prefer to use dried, which can take as little as 20 minutes to cook, depending on the variety and age. *Giardiniera* are preserved mixed vegetables, which can be bought in jars from Italian delis; their crunchy texture and slight sharpness from the vinegar combines perfectly with the lentils. Ensure you buy good-quality firm tomatoes, otherwise you could just add more of the *giardiniera*, if you prefer. Serve with some good rustic bread for a delicious, healthy meal at any time. It can be enjoyed both warm or cold, so is also ideal as a packed lunch or to take on picnics.

Cooking time: 25 minutes

Serves 4

1 cup/7 oz/200 g brown or green lentils
1 garlic clove, left whole and squashed
3 whole thyme sprigs, plus the leaves from
    2 sprigs
7 oz/200 g *giardiniera* (Italian preserved
    vegetables)
8 baby plum tomatoes
⅓ cup/80 ml extra-virgin olive oil
sea salt and freshly ground black pepper

Place the dried lentils in a heavy-based saucepan filled with cold water, together with the squashed garlic clove and 3 whole thyme sprigs. Bring to a boil and simmer for about 20 minutes over medium heat, or until cooked (check the instructions on the package).

Meanwhile, drain the *giardiniera* vegetables and slice the tomatoes.

Drain the lentils, discarding the garlic and thyme, and leave to cool slightly. Place the cooled lentils in a serving dish, together with the *giardiniera* and tomatoes. Add the olive oil and fresh thyme leaves, season with salt and pepper, and mix well.

INSALATA DI SPECK CROCCANTE, MELA VERDE E NOCI

CRISPY SPECK, GREEN APPLE, AND WALNUT SALAD

The slight saltiness of speck combined with the crunchy walnuts and fresh lemony apples makes this a delightful starter or light lunch. Make sure you place the sliced apples in acidulated water first, to avoid them going brown.

Cooking time: 20 minutes

Serves 4

2 tart green apples, such as Granny Smith
juice of 1 lemon
1 romaine lettuce
3½ oz/100 g Italian speck
   (smoked, air-dried ham)
¼ cup/60 ml extra-virgin olive oil
sea salt and freshly ground black pepper
⅓ cup/1¾ oz/50 g coarsely chopped walnuts
⅓ cup/1 oz/30 g shaved Parmesan

Wash the apples, core them, and cut into thin slices. Place the slices in a bowl of acidulated water (water combined with half of the lemon juice) and set aside.

Roughly chop the lettuce and arrange on a serving platter.

Slice the speck into thin strips. Heat 1 tablespoon of the olive oil in a frying pan over medium heat, add the speck slices, and fry, stirring, until crispy, but be careful not to let them burn. Remove and drain on paper towels.

Combine the remaining olive oil with the remaining lemon juice in a large bowl, season with salt and pepper, and whisk with a fork until slightly thickened. Drain the apples well, pat dry with paper towels, and add them to the dressing mixture, tossing well.

Arrange the apples over the lettuce on the platter, pouring over any remaining dressing. Sprinkle on the walnuts and cooked speck, and top with Parmesan shavings.

PROSCIUTTO E MELONE

PROSCIUTTO WITH CANTALOUPE

Preparation time: 10 minutes

Serves 4

1 large cantaloupe
a handful of arugula leaves
1 tbsp extra-virgin olive oil
1½ tsp balsamic vinegar
sea salt
8 slices of prosciutto, about 4½ oz/125 g
8 grissini (breadsticks)

Slice the melon in half and discard the seeds. Slice the melon into segments or chunks. Set aside.

Dress the arugula in the olive oil and balsamic vinegar. Add salt, to taste.

Wrap the prosciutto slices around the grissini.

Arrange the dressed arugula and melon on a large serving platter with the prosciutto-wrapped grissini.

BRUSCHETTE CON PESCHE E PROSCIUTTO

BRUSCHETTA OF PEACHES AND PROSCIUTTO

Cooking time: 12 minutes

Serves 4

scant ½ cup/100 ml white wine
2 tsp sugar
8 fresh mint leaves
2 peaches, quartered
4 slices of rustic bread (any will do,
    but Pugliese-style or sourdough are good)
extra-virgin olive oil, for drizzling
4 slices of prosciutto

Place the white wine, sugar, and 4 of the mint leaves in a small saucepan and place over low–medium heat. Simmer for about 5 minutes, until the mixture reduces by about half. Do not let the mixture boil.

Meanwhile, heat a frying pan or griddle pan over a low–medium heat and lightly toast the peaches for about 5 minutes, turning them over so that all the sides get some color.

Toast the slices of bread, drizzle with a little olive oil, then top with the roasted peaches and prosciutto slices. Finally, drizzle over the reduced wine sauce and garnish with the remaining mint leaves.

MELE E PERE ARROSTO CON PROSCIUTTO

PROSCIUTTO WITH ROASTED APPLES AND PEARS

Cooking time: 25–30 minutes (including prep time)

Serves 4

4 small apples (about 10½ oz/300 g)
2 large pears (about 14 oz/400 g), firm variety
2 rosemary sprigs
6 sage leaves
sea salt and freshly ground black pepper
extra-virgin olive oil
juice of 1 small lemon
2½ tbsp raw pistachios
8 slices of prosciutto, about 4½ oz/125 g

Preheat the oven to 425°F/220°C.

Wash the fruit. Slice the apples into fairly thick rounds and the pears lengthways into 4 quarters, discarding the seeds. Place the fruit in a roasting pan, sprinkle with the herbs and some salt and pepper, and drizzle with the olive oil and lemon juice. Roast in the oven for 15–20 minutes, until cooked through (but not falling apart) and golden.

Meanwhile, roast the pistachios: spread them out on a baking tray and place in the oven for about 5 minutes; or toast in a frying pan over medium heat for about 3 minutes. Set aside to cool, then rub them between thumb and fingers to remove the skins.

Arrange the fruit on a serving dish with the slices of prosciutto, sprinkle with the pistachios, and serve.

SUSINE E FICHI AL FORNO CON PROSCIUTTO

CARAMELIZED PLUMS AND FIGS WITH PROSCIUTTO

Cooking time: 20 minutes (including prep time)

Serves 4–6

4–6 large figs (about 8½ oz/240 g)
4 large plums (about 1 lb 2 oz/500 g)
4 thyme sprigs, leaves only
2 tbsp brown sugar
2 tbsp extra-virgin olive oil,
    plus extra for drizzling
juice of ½ lemon
sea salt and freshly ground black pepper
generous 4 cups (4¼ oz/120 g) mixed baby
    salad greens
2½ tbsp walnuts, coarsely chopped
8–12 slices of prosciutto

Preheat the oven to 450°F/230°C.

Wash and dry the fruit. Slice the figs in half. Remove the pits from the plums and slice them into segments. Place the fruit in a baking dish, sprinkle with the thyme and sugar, and roast in the oven for 10 minutes. Remove from the oven and cool for about 5 minutes.

Meanwhile, combine the olive oil and lemon juice, season with some salt and pepper, and dress the salad greens. Arrange the salad on a large serving platter and top with the warm, caramelized fruit. Scatter with the chopped walnuts and the slices of prosciutto, then drizzle with a little more olive oil before serving.

SOUPS

Soups are simple to prepare, don't need a long time to cook, and provide a nutritious, satisfying meal at any time. They are very versatile—depending on personal taste and the type of soup, they can be served either as they are, with chunky pieces of vegetables or other ingredients, or whizzed to a smooth, creamy consistency. They can also be prepared in advance and gently reheated to serve, or divided into portions and frozen for later. In fact, soups are so easy to prepare, it is often worth making more to put in the freezer, so that you always have a healthy meal on hand on those super-busy days or for when the fridge is bare.

There is something so nourishing and feel-good about homemade soup that eating it always takes me back to my childhood, when we would very often have thick bean soups during the winter. We used to make them with dried beans, which we always kept in our pantry, but these had to be soaked overnight and the cooking time was long. These days, we're lucky to have such a vast range of ready-to-use canned beans and legumes available to us; even vegetables can be bought pre-chopped, so you can have ready-prepared ingredients on hand to create delicious soups in no time.

In Italy, soup is usually served as a *primo* (appetizer) instead of pasta. Depending on when it is served, it could also be a filling bean-and-pasta soup for lunch, or a light broth for the evening meal. I hope you will enjoy making the super-simple soups in this book, which can be eaten both as an appetizer or main course.

MINESTRONE VELOCE

QUICK MINESTRONE SOUP

Packed full of nutritious veggies, this soup is basically vitamins in a bowl! Based on the classic Italian minestrone, I have included borlotti beans and *pastina* (small pasta shapes). If you prefer, you could omit the *pastina*. In fact, you could omit any vegetable you don't like or don't have and replace with others. Most of these vegetables can be bought pre-washed and chopped, saving you time. For added flavor, you could serve with a dollop of Pesto Sauce (see p.184).

Cooking time: 35 minutes (not including vegetable prep)

Serves 4–6

¼ cup/60 ml extra-virgin olive oil
1 large onion, finely chopped
2 celery stalks, finely chopped
2 carrots, finely chopped
1 small fennel bulb, finely chopped
1 zucchini, cut into small chunks
1 large potato, peeled and cut into
    small chunks
10 oz/280 g Savoy cabbage, shredded
6 cherry tomatoes
a handful of fresh basil leaves
6½ cups/1.5 liters vegetable stock
1 × 14-oz/400-g can of borlotti (cranberry or
    roman) beans, drained
⅓ cup/1¾ oz/50 g frozen peas
⅔ cup/2½ oz/75 g small pasta shells (pastina)
sea salt and freshly ground black pepper
grated Parmesan, to serve
Pesto Sauce (see p.184), to serve (optional)

Heat the extra-virgin olive oil in a large heavy-based saucepan set over medium–high heat. Add the onion and celery and sweat for a couple of minutes. Add the carrots, fennel, zucchini, potato, cabbage, tomatoes, and basil, and mix well. Pour in the stock, bring to a boil, then lower the heat and cook for 20 minutes. Add the borlotti beans, peas, and pasta and continue to cook for about 6–8 minutes, until the pasta is cooked (check cooking times on the package).

Remove from the heat, season with salt and pepper to taste, and serve with grated Parmesan and a dollop of pesto, if desired.

ZUPPA PICANTE DI CECI E BIETOLE

SPICY CHICKPEA AND CHARD SOUP

This is one of my favorite soups—I love chickpeas and I adore chili peppers! The hot pepper gives a real kick to the chickpeas and chard. I use one whole fresh red chili pepper in this recipe, but you can adjust according to taste. You could omit it altogether if you prefer or, if cooking for people who don't like spice, just add some red pepper flakes to individual portions at the end. If you can't find Swiss chard, you can substitute spinach, but add this about 5 minutes before the end of the cooking time. Served with toasted bread, this makes a delicious, warming meal.

Cooking time: 25 minutes (not including vegetable prep)

Serves 2 as a main course or 4 as an appetizer

1 tbsp extra-virgin olive oil
1 shallot, finely chopped
½ celery stalk, finely chopped
1 garlic clove, finely chopped
1 fresh red chili pepper, finely chopped
2 cups/6¼ oz/180 g finely chopped Swiss
    chard, stalks and leaves
7 oz/200 g canned chopped tomatoes
1 × 14-oz/400-g can of chickpeas (8½ oz/240 g
    drained weight)
1¾ cups/400 ml hot vegetable stock

To serve:
2–4 slices of rustic bread, such as Pugliese or a
    nice sourdough
1 garlic clove, peeled and left whole
extra-virgin olive oil, for drizzling

Heat the olive oil in a heavy-based saucepan set over medium–high heat. Add the shallot, celery, garlic, and chili pepper, and sweat for a couple of minutes. Stir in the Swiss chard and continue to sweat for 1 minute. Add the tomatoes, chickpeas, and vegetable stock, bring to a boil, then lower the heat to medium, cover with a lid, and simmer for 20 minutes.

Towards the end of the cooking time, grill or toast the slices of bread, rub the garlic clove all over the toasted surface of the bread, and drizzle with a little extra-virgin olive oil.

Divide the soup between individual bowls, drizzle with a little extra-virgin olive oil, and serve with the garlicky toasted bread.

ZUPPA DI FAGIOLI CANNELLINI CON PROSCIUTTO E SPINACI

CANNELLINI BEAN SOUP WITH PROSCIUTTO, SPINACH, AND PARMESAN RIND

The delicate flavor of bay leaves and the slight saltiness of the prosciutto combine perfectly in this feel-good soup. Extremely quick and easy to prepare, it makes a satisfying complete meal served with some good bread, or an equally delicious appetizer. I have not added any salt, since the prosciutto and stock season the soup perfectly, but do check and add to taste, if necessary. For extra flavor, add some coarsely chopped Parmesan rind, which is often added to soups in Italy. If you'd like an extra kick, sprinkle some red pepper flakes in at the end.

Cooking time: 30 minutes

Serves 2 as a main course or 4 as an appetizer

2 tbsp extra-virgin olive oil
2 oz/60 g prosciutto, finely chopped
1 leek, finely chopped
1 small carrot, finely chopped
2 bay leaves
3 cups/700 ml hot vegetable stock
a piece of Parmesan rind (about ¾ oz/20 g),
    coarsely chopped
1 × 14-oz/400-g can of cannellini beans
    (8½ oz/240 g drained weight)
4 cups/4¼ oz/120 g spinach leaves
freshly ground black pepper
freshly grated Parmesan, to serve (optional)

Heat the extra-virgin olive oil in a large heavy-based saucepan set over high heat. Add the prosciutto and fry, stirring, for a couple of minutes, until almost crispy Add the leek, carrot, and bay leaves, then lower the heat to medium and sweat for about 4 minutes. Pour in the stock, add the Parmesan rind, and bring to a boil. Now, lower the heat, cover with a lid, and cook for 15 minutes, stirring from time to time with a wooden spoon, to prevent the Parmesan rind from sticking to the pan. Add the drained cannellini beans and spinach, season with some black pepper, and cook for a further 5 minutes.

Serve with a sprinkling of grated Parmesan, if desired.

ZUPPA DI FAVE AL TIMO CON PANCETTA

THYME-INFUSED FAVA BEAN SOUP WITH CRISPY SMOKED PANCETTA

This is a delicious, creamy soup made using frozen fava beans. The subtle, smoky flavor of the pancetta really comes through and the crispy pancetta gives a nice crunchiness to the dish. It is simply delicious at any time but would make a great appetizer for when you have guests over.

Cooking time: 25–30 minutes

Serves 4

1½ tbsp/¾ oz/20 g butter
1 tbsp extra-virgin olive oil,
    plus an extra splash for frying
5½ oz/150 g smoked pancetta, finely chopped
1 onion, finely chopped
1 celery stalk, finely chopped
1 garlic clove, finely chopped
a handful of thyme leaves,
    plus a few to garnish
2¾ cups/12 oz/350 g frozen shelled fava beans,
    skinned
1 large potato (about 7 oz/200 g), chopped
    into small cubes
4¼ cups/1 liter vegetable stock

Heat the butter and olive oil in a large, heavy-based saucepan set over medium–high heat. Add one-third of the pancetta, and all of the onion, celery, garlic, and thyme, and sweat for 5 minutes. Stir in the fava beans and potato, then pour in the stock and bring to a boil. Reduce the heat, cover with a lid, and simmer for 10–12 minutes, until the beans and potatoes are cooked. Remove from the heat and allow to cool a little.

Meanwhile, add a splash of extra-virgin olive oil to a small frying pan set over medium heat. Add the remaining pancetta and fry, stirring, until nice and crispy. Set aside.

Transfer the slightly cooled soup to a blender or food processor and blend until smooth (you may need to do this in two batches). Return it to the saucepan and gently reheat, if necessary. Divide among individual bowls, sprinkle with the crispy pancetta, and garnish with thyme leaves before serving.

ZUPPA DI FUNGHI

MUSHROOM SOUP

This simple mushroom soup delivers all the flavor of wild mushrooms without the price tag! Reconstituted dried porcini mushrooms are blended with vegetables and served with sautéed cremini mushrooms and pancetta. If you like, you could use a selection of wild fungi in season and, for vegetarians, omit the pancetta. Dried porcini are obtainable from all good Italian delis and larger supermarkets.

Cooking time: 25 minutes (including prep)

Serves 4

1 oz/30 g dried porcini mushrooms
¼ cup/60 ml extra-virgin olive oil,
   plus extra for drizzling
1 large onion, finely chopped
1 celery stalk, finely chopped
1 large carrot, finely chopped
2 rosemary sprigs, needles only
2 garlic cloves, finely chopped
3¼ cups/750 ml vegetable stock
1½ tbsp/¾ oz/20 g butter
1¾ oz/50 g pancetta, cubed
2 cups/6¼ oz/180 g cremini
   mushrooms, sliced
sea salt

Place the dried porcini in a bowl, pour over warm water to cover, and leave to soften while you prepare the vegetables.

Heat 3 tablespoons of the olive oil in a large saucepan set over medium heat. Add the onion, celery, carrot, half of the rosemary, and half of the garlic, and sweat for about 3 minutes. Drain the porcini (reserving the soaking water), roughly chop, add to the pan, and continue to sweat for 2 minutes. Add the porcini soaking liquid and vegetable stock and simmer for 8 minutes.

Meanwhile, heat the butter and 1 tablespoon of the olive oil in a frying pan set over medium heat. Add the pancetta and the remaining rosemary and garlic, and sweat for 1 minute. Add the cremini mushrooms, season with some salt, and sauté for about 5–6 minutes, until the mushrooms are nicely browned all over.

Put the vegetables and stock into a food processor or blender and blend to a smooth consistency. Divide among 4 soup bowls, top with the sautéed mushrooms and pancetta, drizzle with a little olive oil, and serve.

ZUPPA ALLA ZUCCA E PATATA DOLCE
SQUASH AND SWEET POTATO SOUP WITH GARLIC AND ROSEMARY

Warming and comforting, this is my go-to soup during the fall and winter, when squash is in season. You can use butternut or onion squash, or even pumpkin—it's your choice. I like the addition of sweet potato too, for its excellent nutritional value. Rosemary and chili peppers are good partners to all types of squash and sweet potato, but I have left the chili pepper optional (although when I make it, I like to add more chili and make it nice and spicy!). Sometimes, when I am making this for the family, I omit the chili during cooking and just add red pepper flakes to my portion at the end.

This soup is really simple to prepare and takes no time to cook. The only part that takes a little time is the peeling and chopping of the squash. You can do this in advance, if you wish, and store the chunks in the refrigerator. You can also buy ready-peeled chunks of squash and sweet potato in supermarkets now!

Cooking time: 25–30 minutes (not including vegetable prep)

Serves 4–6

2 tbsp extra-virgin olive oil,
    plus extra for drizzling
3 garlic cloves, finely chopped
1 onion, finely chopped
2 rosemary sprigs, needles only
½ fresh red chili pepper (optional)
6 cups/1 lb 12 oz/800 g peeled and cubed
    squash
7 oz/200 g peeled and cubed sweet potato
5 cups/1.2 liters hot vegetable stock

Heat the olive oil in a large, heavy-based saucepan set over medium heat. Add the garlic, onion, rosemary, and chili (if using) and sweat for about 4 minutes. Stir in the squash and sweet potato, then increase the heat and add the hot stock. Bring to a boil, then reduce the heat and cook for 12–15 minutes, until the squash and sweet potato are soft and cooked through. Remove from the heat and allow to cool a little.

Transfer the slightly cooled soup to a blender or food processor and blend until smooth (you may need to do this in 2 batches). Return the soup to the saucepan and gently reheat, if necessary. Divide among bowls and serve with a drizzle of extra-virgin olive oil.

CREMA DI FAGIOLI CON PESTO DI OLIVE

CREAMY BLACK-EYED PEA SOUP WITH OLIVE PESTO

This is a delicious, creamy soup that goes really well with the crunchy olive pesto. Make sure you get good-quality green olives, such as the Gaeta or Nocellara varieties (these, however, don't come pitted, so you will have to do this yourself—you can easily do it while the soup is cooking). Quick and simple to prepare, this would make a lovely appetizer when you have guests or, of course, at any time.

Cooking time: 25 minutes (not including vegetable prep)

Serves 2–4

2 tbsp extra-virgin olive oil
1 shallot, finely chopped
½ leek, finely chopped
1 garlic clove, finely chopped
1 small carrot, finely chopped
½ small fennel bulb, finely chopped
leaves of 1 thyme sprig
1 × 14-oz/400-g can of black-eyed
    peas, drained
2½ cups/600 ml vegetable stock
sea salt and freshly ground black pepper

For the pesto:
1¼ cups/4½ oz/125 g pitted green olives
a handful of parsley
1 garlic clove
1 tsp capers
2 tbsp extra-virgin olive oil

Heat the olive oil in a large, heavy-based saucepan set over medium heat. Add the shallot, leek, garlic, carrot, fennel, and thyme, and sweat for about 4 minutes. Stir in the drained black-eyed peas and cook for 1 minute to let the flavors infuse. Pour in the stock, increase the heat, and bring to a boil. Now reduce the heat, cover with a lid, and cook for 15 minutes. Season with salt and pepper, remove from the heat, and allow to cool a little.

Meanwhile, make the pesto. Whizz all the ingredients in a food processor or blender, until well combined but retaining a crunchy texture. Set aside.

Transfer the slightly cooled soup to a blender or food processor and blend until smooth (you may need to do this in 2 batches). Return it to the saucepan and gently reheat, if necessary. Divide among bowls and serve with a generous dollop of the olive pesto.

ZUPPA DI PESCE VELOCE
QUICK FISH SOUP

This speedy soup is perfect for any fish lover who doesn't want to spend ages cleaning shellfish! Buy ready-peeled jumbo shrimp and ask your fishmonger to slice the squid and even chop the cod, if you're pressed for time. You can even buy the veggies ready-chopped too! This dish of delicate seafood, cooked in tomatoes and served with toasted bread, makes a delicious main course.

Cooking time: 20 minutes (not including prep)

Serves 4

¼ cup/60 ml extra-virgin olive oil,
    plus extra for drizzling
3 banana shallots, very finely chopped
2 celery stalks, very finely chopped
2 small carrots, very finely chopped
½ fresh red chili pepper, finely chopped
2 bay leaves
10 raw jumbo shrimp
7 oz/200 g cleaned squid, sliced into rings
7 oz/200 g cod, cut into small chunks
scant ½ cup/100 ml white wine
2⅓ cups/1 lb 5 oz/600 g tomato passata
    or purée
sea salt
a handful fresh parsley, finely chopped
slices of toasted rustic bread, to serve

Heat the olive oil in a medium-size, heavy-based saucepan set over medium heat. Add the vegetables, chili pepper, and bay leaves and sweat for about 2 minutes. Stir in the shrimp and squid, and continue to cook for a further 3 minutes. Add the cod and cook for 1 minute. Pour in the white wine, increase the heat, and allow the alcohol to cook off for a minute or so. Carefully remove the cod chunks and set aside. Add the tomato passata, together with a scant ½ cup/ 100 ml of water and some salt to taste, lower the heat, then cover with a lid, and cook for 10 minutes.

Return the cod to the pan and heat through for a final minute. Remove from the heat and serve sprinkled with the chopped parsley, a drizzle of extra-virgin olive oil, and with the toasted bread on the side.

PASTA

I don't think I know anyone who dislikes pasta. Universally loved, it is certainly a dish that Italians enjoy on a daily basis—for some, a meal would be incomplete without it!

Pasta is healthy, nutritious, and versatile. It's so quick to cook—for me, pasta is "fast food" at its best. Even the pasta sauces are uncomplicated and just as speedy to make. In fact, most of the sauces in this book are cooked while the pasta is boiling. You can also make some sauces in advance and freeze them for later. A simple, classic tomato sauce is worth making lots of and freezing it in batches for later use. On those weeknights when time is really precious, you can rest assured that you have a good home-cooked meal on hand, which can be whipped up in no time at all.

Italians are passionate about their pasta and insist that only certain shapes go with certain sauces. Long pasta, such as spaghetti or linguine, tends to accompany light tomato or fish sauces. And short pasta shapes, such as penne or farfalle, go well with more robust-tasting, meaty sauces. It is for this reason that Italians keep a vast selection of pasta shapes in their pantries—when I visit my sister in Italy, I'm always amazed by how many different packages she has, and she lives by herself!

I like to keep both long and short shapes on hand, as well as smaller shapes to add to soups. Spaghetti is a must in my pantry, because it is so easy to make a meal with, even when the fridge is bare. A simple sauce of *aglio, olio e peperoncino* (garlic, extra-virgin olive oil, and chili pepper) makes a quick meal at any time. For a milder flavor, my daughter Olivia's favorite is spaghetti with melted butter and Parmesan; it was always a winner when she was a toddler, and now, as a teen, she will often prepare it herself.

Pasta is also good for you. It is an ideal carbohydrate, since it releases energy slowly, is easily digestible, and its lack of fat makes it suitable for low-calorie diets (bearing in mind what goes into the sauce, of course!). You can be sure you are serving a good, nutritious meal made in no time.

MAFALDA CORTA CON SPINACI E MASCARPONE

CREAMY MASCARPONE AND SPINACH PASTA

For this quick and easy pasta dish, I have used a short-shaped pasta called *mafalda corta*, but you could substitute with farfalle or fusilli. The lemon zest added at the end gives the dish a lovely, fresh flavor.

Cooking time: 12–15 minutes

Serves 4

11¼ oz/320 g *mafalda corta* pasta
sea salt, for the cooking water
1½ tbsp/¾ oz/20 g butter
1 garlic clove, slightly squashed
5½ cups/5½ oz/150 g baby spinach leaves
¾ cup/6 oz/175 g mascarpone
¼ cup/¾ oz/20 g grated Parmesan
freshly ground black pepper, to serve
zest of 1 small, unwaxed, organic lemon,
    to serve

Bring a large saucepan of salted water to a boil and cook the *mafalda corta* pasta for 8–10 minutes, until *al dente* (check the instructions on your package).

Meanwhile, melt the butter in a large frying pan over medium heat, add the garlic, and allow to infuse for 1 minute. Stir in the spinach, cover with a lid, and cook for a couple of minutes, until the spinach has wilted. Discard the garlic.

In a bowl, mix the mascarpone and Parmesan, adding some salt and pepper to taste, until you obtain a creamy consistency. Add this to the cooked spinach and gently heat through.

Drain the pasta, reserving some of the cooking water. Add the pasta to the creamy spinach sauce, mixing well to combine, and adding a little of the cooking water, if necessary. Remove from the heat and serve with some freshly ground black pepper and a little grated lemon zest.

BUCATINI ALLA GRICIA

BUCATINI WITH PORK AND PECORINO

Along with its cousins, *carbonara*, *amatriciana*, and *cacio e pepe*, this dish forms the backbone of Roman cooking. Using the typically favored Roman ingredients of *guanciale* instead of pancetta, and Pecorino instead of Parmesan, this simple dish is often what locals cook when they need to make a quick meal. *Guanciale* is cured pork cheek—it has an intense flavor and is especially used in robust traditional Roman cuisine. It can be found in good Italian delis, and it can also be substituted with good-quality pancetta.

Cooking time: 15 minutes

Serves 4

11¼ oz/320 g *bucatini* pasta
sea salt, for the cooking water
7 oz/200 g *guanciale* or pancetta
2 tbsp extra-virgin olive oil
plenty of freshly ground black pepper
scant 1 cup/2 oz/60 g grated Pecorino

Bring a large saucepan of salted water to a boil and cook the pasta until *al dente* (check the instructions on your package for cooking time).

Meanwhile, chop the *guanciale* into small cubes or thin strips. Heat the olive oil in a frying pan set over medium heat, add the *guanciale*, and fry, stirring, for a couple of minutes, until the pork is cooked through with a nice golden color (be careful not to burn it!). Season with plenty of black pepper and add a ladle of the pasta cooking water, continuing to cook. When the pasta is ready, drain (reserving some of the cooking water) and add to the sauce. Mix well, then stir in the grated Pecorino and a little of the reserved pasta water, if necessary.

Serve immediately, with plenty of black pepper.

FARFALLE CON ASPARAGI E FUNGHI CON PANCETTA

FARFALLE PASTA WITH ASPARAGUS, MUSHROOMS, AND CRISPY PANCETTA

Quick, nutritious, and delicious, this pasta dish makes a substantial main course. If you're catering for vegetarians, just omit the crispy pancetta. For speed, buy ready-trimmed green beans, asparagus tips, and ready-sliced mushrooms.

Cooking time: 20 minutes

Serves 4

8½ oz/240 g trimmed green beans
7 oz/200 g asparagus tips
sea salt, for the cooking water
14 oz/400 g farfalle pasta
4¼ oz/120 g pancetta or bacon slices
¼ cup/60 ml extra-virgin olive oil,
    plus extra for drizzling
2 large shallots, finely chopped
1½ cups/3½ oz/100 g thinly sliced mushrooms
sea salt and freshly ground black pepper

Preheat the broiler to high.

Cook the green beans and asparagus in a saucepan of boiling water for about 5 minutes, until tender. Drain and set aside.

Bring a large saucepan of salted water to a boil and cook the farfalle pasta for 10–12 minutes, until *al dente* (check the instructions on your package).

Meanwhile, place the pancetta or bacon slices under the hot broiler, and cook on both sides until crispy, about 2–3 minutes per side. Set aside.

In a large frying pan set over medium heat, heat the olive oil, add the shallots, and sweat for a couple of minutes. Add the mushrooms and fry, stirring, for a minute or so. Add the cooked green beans and asparagus, some salt and pepper to taste, and a couple of tablespoons of the pasta's hot cooking water, and cook for 2–3 minutes.

Drain the pasta, reserving a little of the cooking water. Add the pasta to the pan with the vegetables, turn the heat up to high, and mix well to combine, adding a little of the pasta water to loosen the sauce, if necessary.

Serve garnished with the crispy pancetta, a grind of black pepper, and a drizzle of olive oil.

PENNE INTEGRALI CON BROCCOLI E PATATA DOLCE

WHOLE-GRAIN PENNE WITH BROCCOLI AND SWEET POTATO

Pasta with broccoli is a common dish in Italy, where it is usually flavored with garlic and chili pepper. In this recipe, the broccoli is mashed in a blender and served with small chunks of delicious sweet potato, adding extra nutrients and color to the dish. It makes a healthy combination that goes really well with wholewheat pasta. If you prefer, you can substitute the whole-grain penne with white-flour penne.

Cooking time: 20 minutes (not including prep)

Serves 4

11¼ oz/320 g whole-grain penne
sea salt, for the cooking water
14 oz/400 g broccoli florets
9 oz/250 g sweet potato, cut into cubes
sea salt, for the cooking water
3 tbsp extra-virgin olive oil,
    plus an extra splash
2 garlic cloves, finely chopped
½ fresh red chili pepper, finely chopped
scant 1 cup/2 oz/60 g grated Parmesan, plus
    extra for sprinkling, if desired

Bring a large saucepan of salted water to a boil and add the pasta, broccoli, and sweet potato. Cook until the broccoli is tender, 4–5 minutes. Remove the broccoli with a slotted spoon and set aside to drain in a colander. Continue to cook the pasta and sweet potato, until the pasta is *al dente*, 8–10 minutes (check the instructions on your package).

Meanwhile, heat the olive oil in a large frying pan over medium heat, add the garlic and chili, and sweat for about 30 seconds. Add the drained broccoli and fry, stirring, for 1 minute or so.

Remove from the heat and transfer the broccoli mixture to a food processor. Add a further splash of olive oil and the grated Parmesan and blend until smooth. Return the mixture to the frying pan.

Drain the pasta and sweet potato, reserving some of the cooking water. Add to the broccoli mixture, mix well, and heat through, adding a little of the reserved cooking water, if needed.

Serve with an extra sprinkling of Parmesan, if desired.

LA PASTA AL PESCE DI MICHAEL

MICHAEL'S FISHY PASTA

This is my eldest son Michael's recipe—he often cooks quick dishes such as this. He was very excited when I told him of this book, since he is always looking for fast, nutritious meals to cook for himself and his partner, Sebastian, when they both return home after a long day's work. Served with perhaps a green side-salad, this wonderfully speedy and healthy dish is a complete meal.

Cooking time: 20 minutes

Serves 2 as a main course

sea salt
3 tbsp extra-virgin olive oil
1 large garlic clove, finely chopped
½ fresh red chili pepper, finely chopped
3 anchovy fillets
1 tsp salted capers, rinsed
1 × 14-oz/400-g can of plum tomatoes,
    drained, reserving 1 tbsp of the juice
a handful of fresh parsley, coarsely chopped
5½ oz/150 g cod, skin-on, cut into "fingers"
7 oz/200 g linguine

Place a large saucepan of salted water on the heat to boil.

In a large, deep frying pan, heat the olive oil over medium heat, add the garlic, chili, and anchovy fillets and sweat for 1 minute or so, until the anchovy fillets melt. Stir in the capers, tomatoes, a quarter of the parsley, and some salt to taste. Increase the heat and cook for 2 minutes. Add the cod pieces, skin-side down, reduce the heat to medium, add another quarter of the parsley, cover with a lid, and cook for 10 minutes. Remove the fish pieces and set aside.

When the pasta water has come to a boil, add the linguine and cook until *al dente* (check the instructions on your package for cooking time). Drain, reserving a little of the cooking water.

Add the drained pasta to the tomato sauce and mix together, adding a little of the reserved cooking water, until well combined. Remove from the heat, stir in the remaining parsley, and serve with the cod pieces on top.

CAVATELLI CON SALSICCA, FUNGHI E POMODORI SECCHI

CAVATELLI PASTA WITH SAUSAGE, MUSHROOMS, AND SUN-DRIED TOMATOES

For this recipe, get the best Italian pork sausages you can (obtainable from Italian delis); both fennel- or garlic-infused sausages work well. Also, try to get good-quality sun-dried tomatoes, preferably ones that are not preserved in oil (also available at good grocery stores or Italian delis). If the tomatoes are in oil, then drain well, patting them dry with paper towels. *Cavatelli* are a small, hollow pasta shape from southern Italy, made from durum wheat semolina flour and water. This dish has all the flavors of rural Italy and makes a delicious complete meal.

Cooking time: 15 minutes (not including prep)

Serves 4

11¼ oz/320 g *cavatelli* pasta
sea salt, for the cooking water
¼ cup/60 ml extra-virgin olive oil
1 garlic clove, finely chopped
3 thyme sprigs
4 sun-dried tomatoes, finely chopped
12 oz/350 g Italian pork sausages, skinned
   and crumbled
scant ½ cup/100 ml white wine
3½ cups/12 oz/350 g mushrooms, thinly sliced
generous ½ cup/1½ oz/40 g shaved Parmesan,
   to serve

Bring a large saucepan of salted water to a boil and cook the pasta until *al dente* (check the instructions on your package for cooking time).

Meanwhile, heat the olive oil in a large frying pan over medium heat, add the garlic, 2 of the thyme sprigs, and the sun-dried tomatoes, and sweat for 1 minute. Add the crumbled-up sausage meat and fry, stirring, for a few minutes, until lightly browned. Increase the heat to high, add the white wine, and allow the alcohol to cook off for a minute or so. Stir in the mushrooms and the remaining thyme sprig, then lower the heat, cover with a lid, and cook for 10 minutes. Add a little of the hot pasta water to stop it from drying up, if necessary.

Drain the pasta, reserving a little cooking water. Add the pasta and reserved water to the sausage and mushroom sauce, mix well to combine, and serve with shavings of Parmesan.

FUSILLI BUCATI CON PANNA, NOCI E BRICCIOLE CROCCANTI

FUSILLI BUCATI WITH WALNUTS, CREAM, AND CRISPY CROUTONS

This creamy pasta dish goes really well with walnuts and celery. Do ensure you buy celery with lots of leaves and use the tender heart or the middle of the celery. In rural southern Italy, it was quite common to use breadcrumbs (from leftover bread) to top pasta dishes when cheese was unavailable, hence the idea of crispy croutons in this recipe. Quick and simple to prepare, this makes a deliciously different pasta dish.

Cooking time: 15 minutes (not including prep)

Serves 4

11¼ oz/320 g *fusilli bucati* pasta
sea salt and freshly ground black pepper
1 garlic clove, peeled
1 celery heart with leaves, stalks thinly sliced
⅔ cup/3¼ oz/90 g walnuts
3 tbsp milk
a pinch of nutmeg
2 oz/60 g day-old bread, cut into small cubes
scant ½ cup/100 ml light cream
1 tbsp extra-virgin olive oil

Bring a large saucepan of salted water to a boil and cook the pasta for 10–12 minutes, until *al dente* (check the instructions on your package).

Meanwhile, in a food processor, combine the garlic, celery leaves, walnuts, milk, nutmeg, half of the bread cubes, and some salt and pepper, and process until smooth. Add the cream last and mix together. If the sauce is a little thick, add a little of the pasta water. Set aside.

In a large frying pan, heat the olive oil over medium heat. Add the sliced celery stalks and the remaining bread cubes and fry, stirring, for a minute or so, until golden.

Drain the pasta, reserving a little of the cooking water. Add the creamy sauce to a large saucepan set over a low heat and warm through. Add the pasta and, if necessary, a little of the reserved cooking water to the sauce, and stir to combine. Divide among plates and top with the crispy croutons and celery.

GNOCCHI CON GORGONZOLA E PERA

GNOCCHI WITH GORGONZOLA AND PEAR

Classic gnocchi and Gorgonzola are the perfect combination. The addition of sweet, ripe pears here really enhances the flavor, making this a delicious, speedy meal. Try to get good-quality gnocchi from an Italian deli; I really like the small variety, sometimes known as *chicchi*.

Cooking time: 10 minutes

Serves 4

3 tbsp/1½ oz/40 g butter
2 thyme sprigs, leaves only
1 ripe Bosc pear, peeled and cut into small
    chunks
7 oz/200 g Gorgonzola, coarsely chopped
⅓ cup/80 ml milk
a pinch of grated nutmeg, plus extra to serve
1 lb 2 oz/500 g pack of ready-made gnocchi
sea salt

Place a large saucepan of water on the heat to boil.

In a large frying pan, melt the butter over medium heat, add the thyme leaves and pear chunks, and fry, stirring, for about 30 seconds. Stir in the Gorgonzola, add the milk and nutmeg, and stir well until the cheese melts. Turn the heat down to low.

When the water in the saucepan is boiling, drop in the gnocchi and cook for 1–2 minutes, until the gnocchi float to the top. At this point, use a slotted spoon to transfer the gnocchi into the creamy sauce and mix well to combine. Add a little salt to taste, remove from the heat, and serve immediately with a little extra grated nutmeg.

TROFIE AL PESTO CON NOCI E POMODORO

TROFIE WITH PESTO, WALNUTS, AND TOMATO

Classic Ligurian *trofie al pesto* is now a popular pasta dish all over Italy and further afield. I remember when I first discovered *trofie* (short, thin, twisted eggless pasta) on a trip to the region in the 1990s—they were then unheard of outside of Italy. I am pleased to say that, over the years, good Italian delis, and now some supermarkets, have started stocking it internationally. *Trofie* take a little longer to cook than most other pasta shapes, so it's important to check the cooking instructions on your package. I usually like to make my own pesto (see recipe on p.184), but you can find good-quality fresh pesto at Italian delis, as well as some excellent varieties in jars, which make great pantry essentials. Here, the addition of walnuts and tomatoes makes this quick and simple dish a very tasty and nutritious meal.

Cooking time: 15–20 minutes (depending on pasta cooking time)

Serves 4

11¼ oz/320 g *trofie* pasta
sea salt, for the cooking water
3½ oz/100 g Pesto Sauce (see p.184)
a splash of extra-virgin olive oil
⅓ cup/1½ oz/40 g walnut pieces
2 tomatoes (about 9 oz/250 g), deseeded and
   coarsely chopped
a few basil leaves, to garnish
grated Parmesan, to serve

Bring a large saucepan of salted water to the boil, add the *trofie*, and cook for 12–15 minutes, until *al dente* (check the instructions on your package).

Meanwhile, make ready the other ingredients.

When the pasta is nearly cooked, place the pesto in a large frying pan with a splash of extra-virgin olive oil and gently heat through. Drain the *trofie*, reserving a little cooking water. Add the *trofie* and reserved cooking water to the pesto sauce and mix well. Stir in the walnuts and tomatoes, remove from the heat, and serve, garnished with basil leaves and some grated Parmesan, if desired.

CARBONARA DI SALMONE AFFUMICATO

SMOKED SALMON CARBONARA

This is a twist on classic carbonara, using smoked salmon instead of pancetta. You can buy smoked salmon trimmings, which are not only more economical but are already in small pieces, which saves on chopping time. Simple and nutritious, I'm sure this will become a favorite mid-week supper when time is precious! Though cheese doesn't typically go with fish, I quite like a little grated Pecorino sprinkled on mine, but have left it optional.

Cooking time: 10 minutes (including prep!)

Serves 4

11¼ oz/320 g spaghetti or linguine
sea salt and freshly ground black pepper
2 egg yolks
1 tbsp milk
1½ tbsp/¾ oz/20 g butter
3 tbsp extra-virgin olive oil
2 bay leaves
7 oz/200 g smoked salmon trimmings
3 tbsp white wine
a little grated Pecorino, to serve (optional)

Bring a large saucepan of salted water to a boil and cook the pasta until *al dente* (check the instructions on your package for cooking time).

While the pasta is cooking, lightly beat the egg yolks in a bowl with the milk and some salt and pepper, and set aside.

In a large frying pan, heat the butter and olive oil over medium heat. Add the bay leaves and sweat for 1 minute. Add the smoked salmon trimmings and fry, stirring, for a couple of minutes to heat through. Add the white wine and allow the alcohol to cook off for a minute or so. Season with black pepper.

Drain the pasta, add it to the frying pan with the smoked salmon, and mix well. Remove from the heat, pour in the egg mixture, and mix well to combine. Serve with a little grated Pecorino, if desired.

TAGLIOLINI CON PISELLI E RICOTTA

TAGLIOLINI PASTA WITH PEAS AND RICOTTA

A very simple dish of pasta with peas, with the added creaminess of ricotta, this makes a perfect, quick supper for the whole family. You could substitute the *tagliolini* (which are like a thin version of tagliatelle) with linguine, or even short pasta shapes such as farfalle. It's delicious whichever pasta you use!

Cooking time: 12–15 minutes

Serves 4

11¼ oz/320 g *tagliolini* pasta
sea salt, for the cooking water
2 tbsp extra-virgin olive oil
1 small onion, finely chopped
½ handful of basil leaves
1½ cups/7 oz/200 g frozen peas
scant 1 cup/200 ml vegetable stock
1 cup/9 oz/250 g ricotta
freshly ground black pepper

Bring a large saucepan of salted water to a boil and cook the pasta until *al dente* (check the instructions on your package for cooking time).

Meanwhile, heat the olive oil in a large frying pan over medium heat, add the onion and a couple of the basil leaves, and sweat for 2 minutes. Stir in the peas, the remaining basil leaves, and the vegetable stock, and cook for about 3 minutes, until the peas are tender.

In a bowl, combine the ricotta with a little freshly ground black pepper, and mash with a fork.

Drain the pasta, add it to the peas, then stir in the ricotta, and cook for 1 minute or so, until nicely combined and heated through. Serve immediately.

LINGUINE CON ZUCCHINI E GAMBERETTI

LINGUINE WITH ZUCCHINI AND SHRIMP

Shrimp and zucchini combine really well and, added to this speedy and simple pasta dish, makes a delicious, balanced meal. I like to grate zucchini—it's really quick and easy and you can do this while waiting for the pasta water to boil. However, to save more time, you can now buy them ready-spiralized and then give them a quick additional chop.

Cooking time: 20 minutes

Serves 4

14 oz/400 g linguine
sea salt
3 zucchini, about 1 lb 5 oz/600 g
    (6 cups if buying ready-grated/spiralized)
⅓ cup/80 ml extra-virgin olive oil
3 garlic cloves, finely sliced
4 anchovy fillets
10½ oz/300 g peeled shrimp
a handful of basil leaves
juice of ½ lemon, to serve (optional)

Bring a large saucepan of salted water to a boil and cook the pasta until *al dente* (check the instructions on your package for cooking time).

Meanwhile, grate the zucchini (if necessary) on the larger holes of a grater. Taking handfuls of the grated zucchini, squeeze out the excess water and set aside.

Heat the olive oil in a large frying pan set over low–medium heat. Add the garlic and anchovy fillets and sweat for 1 minute or so, until the anchovies have dissolved. Lower the heat if necessary to ensure that you do not burn the garlic. Add the grated zucchini and fry, stirring, for 2–3 minutes, until softened. Season with salt, to taste. Stir in the shrimp and continue to cook for a further 2 minutes.

Drain the pasta, reserving a little of the cooking water, and add it to the sauce in the pan, tossing to combine. Stir in the basil and continue to cook for 1 minute, adding a little of the pasta cooking water if necessary. Serve immediately, with a squeeze of lemon juice to taste, if you like.

TROMPETTI CON CASTAGNE
TROMPETTI PASTA WITH CHESTNUTS

This is a simple, hearty pasta dish made with one of my favorite foods. I love chestnuts—every fall, I love to pick them and am quite happy to have a bowlful for dinner! Although chestnuts are easy to cook—I usually boil them with a bay leaf—you can find vacuum-packed, pre-cooked chestnuts in delis and good supermarkets. Once food for the poor, this versatile ingredient is now quite a delicacy, but it's so nutritious and combines really well with the creamy mascarpone.

Cooking time: 20 minutes

Serves 4

12¾ oz/360 g *trompetti* pasta
sea salt and freshly ground black pepper
¼ cup/60 ml extra-virgin olive oil
1 leek, finely chopped
2¾ oz/80 g pancetta, finely chopped
10½ oz/300 g cooked chestnuts,
    coarsely chopped
2 rosemary sprigs, needles only
⅔ cup/5 oz/140 g mascarpone
grated Pecorino, to serve

Bring a large saucepan of salted water to a boil and cook the *trompetti* pasta for 10–12 minutes, until *al dente* (check the instructions on your package).

Meanwhile, heat the olive oil in a large, deep frying pan over medium heat. Add the leek and pancetta and sweat for a couple of minutes. Stir in the cooked chestnuts, rosemary, and some salt and pepper, cover with the lid, and cook for 5 minutes.

In a bowl, combine the mascarpone with a little of the pasta's hot cooking water to loosen it up a bit, and mix until creamy.

Drain the pasta, reserving a little of the cooking water. Add the pasta to the chestnut sauce, stir in the creamy mascarpone, and mix well, adding a little of the reserved cooking water, if necessary.

Serve with a sprinkling of grated Pecorino.

ORECCHIETTE CON SALSA AL POMODORO E RICOTTA SALATA

ORECCHIETTE PASTA WITH TOMATO AND RICOTTA SALATA

Ricotta salata is a hard version of the creamy cheese we are so familiar with; it is pressed, salted, dried, and aged, and is perfect for grating over pasta dishes such as this one. *Orecchiette*, or "little ears," is an eggless, handmade pasta from Puglia, which can be bought dried. If you don't want to make your own tomato sauce, or don't have any handy, buy a good-quality ready-made one. In fact, you can get all the ingredients for this recipe from a good Italian deli or grocery store. Quick and easy to prepare, this dish is Italian simplicity at its best!

Cooking time: 15 minutes

Serves 4

14 oz/400 g *orecchiette* pasta
sea salt, for the cooking water
½ quantity Basic Tomato Sauce (see p.183)
¾ cup/2¾ oz/80 g grated *ricotta salata*
a few basil leaves, to garnish

Bring a large saucepan of salted water to a boil and cook the *orecchiette* pasta for about 12 minutes, until *al dente* (check the instructions on your package).

Meanwhile, in a large saucepan, gently heat through the tomato sauce.

Drain the pasta and toss through the tomato sauce. Divide among your serving bowls, sprinkle with the grated *ricotta salata*, and garnish with basil leaves.

PASTA AL FORNO AI 4 FORMAGGI

MINI ITALIAN MAC 'N' CHEESE

This is the Italian way of preparing mac 'n' cheese, without the need to make a béchamel sauce. Quick and simple to prepare, it's a great way to use up leftover cheese. You can use a mixture of any cheeses you have in the refrigerator, which is great around the holidays when you might have a lot. Served in individual ramekins, this nutritious, child-friendly dish will be everyone's midweek family favorite.

Cooking time: 15 minutes (including prep)

Serves 4

butter, for greasing
11¼ oz/320 g pasta shapes, either *maccheroni*
   or *spirallini*
sea salt and freshly ground black pepper
2½ oz/70 g Emmental
2¾ oz/80 g Fontal (a type of Fontina
   cheese that is less oily when melted)
   or sharp Cheddar
3½ oz/100 g Gorgonzola
3 tbsp milk
generous ½ cup/1½ oz/40 g grated Parmesan,
   plus extra for sprinkling

Lightly grease 4 individual ramekins with butter. Preheat the broiler to high.

Bring a large saucepan of salted water to a boil and cook the pasta for 10–12 minutes, until *al dente* (check the instructions on your package).

Meanwhile, roughly chop the Emmental, Fontal, and Gorgonzola cheeses. Place them in a large saucepan with the milk, and melt over low heat, stirring with a wooden spoon, until you obtain a creamy consistency.

Drain the pasta and mix it into the creamy cheese sauce, stirring in the grated Parmesan, and adding some salt and pepper, to taste. Divide among the ramekins, top with some extra grated Parmesan, and place under the hot broiler for 4–5 minutes, until golden-brown.

LASAGNE AL PANE CARASAU

TOMATO AND RICOTTA LASAGNE WITH PANE CARASAU

Sardinian *pane carasau* is more than just a simple flatbread and can be made into a variety of succulent dishes, such as this quick lasagne. Use the crispy bread as you would lasagne sheets; don't worry if it breaks—you will need to break the sheets to fit your dish. This thin crispbread is not only quicker to cook than pasta sheets, but the result is a much lighter dish with all the flavor of a normal lasagne. If you don't have time to make your own tomato sauce or don't have any handy, just pick some up ready-made from a good Italian deli. The use of ricotta, much loved in southern Italian baked pasta dishes, makes a quick and light alternative to béchamel sauce.

Cooking time: 30 minutes (including prep)

Serves 4

1 cup/9 oz/250 g ricotta
⅓ cup/1 oz/30 g grated Parmesan,
    plus extra for sprinkling
1 tbsp milk
sea salt and freshly ground black pepper
1 quantity of Basic Tomato Sauce (see p.183)
4¼ oz/120 g *pane carasau* (from your local
    Italian deli)
a handful of basil leaves
4¼ oz/120 g mozzarella, coarsely chopped

Preheat the oven to 400°F/200°C.

Combine the ricotta, Parmesan, and milk, season with some salt and pepper, and mix until creamy.

Line a baking dish with a little of the tomato sauce. Top with a piece of *pane carasau*, followed by another layer of tomato sauce, then a layer of the ricotta mixture. Scatter over a few basil leaves and some of the mozzarella. Continue making layers like this until you use all the ingredients up, ending with a final layer of tomato sauce, scattered with some mozzarella and topped with a sprinkling of grated Parmesan. Bake in the hot oven for 15 minutes.

Once baked, place the lasagne under a hot broiler for about 3 minutes, until golden brown and bubbling.

RISOTTOS

In Italy, risotto has always been the staple food of the northern regions, where rice fields dominate the flat plains of the Po Valley. In traditional northern Italian families, a plate of risotto is served as a *primo* (appetizer) in place of pasta. It's strange—though I was brought up in the south, where pasta ruled, my mother would often cook a type of risotto with plenty of vegetables, especially on the days when she was busy and didn't have time to cook a lot.

Like pasta, risotto is nutritious, versatile, simple to prepare, and quick to cook, often all in one pot! And, like pasta, if your cupboard is bare, a simple, basic risotto with butter and Parmesan makes nourishing comfort food. You can really add whatever ingredients you like to a risotto—my favorite is probably one with lots of veggies. The base of the risotto is usually made simply with a little finely chopped onion, and then I like to add whatever veggies I have—our family favorites are carrots and peas, which we always have on hand.

Risotto can also be made to impress, turning this humble grain into a meal fit for a king. Adding a little truffle butter or oil topped with shavings of truffle can be a real treat. Risotto rice goes so well with this highly prized fungus that in the regions of Italy where it is found—Piemonte, Umbria, Tuscany—it is typical to see this dish on the menus of local restaurants and trattorias.

The secret to a good risotto is the rice. Don't try to make risotto with any old rice because it just won't work. Try to buy the best you can afford—Italian delis will stock Carnaroli, Vialone Nano, or a good Arborio. These short-grain varieties absorb liquid and release starch, making them ideal for creamy risottos. A good stock is important too, and I find a high-quality bouillon cube diluted in hot water to be perfectly adequate. Once made, keep the stock hot by placing it in a pan over low heat and gradually add a ladle or two at a time to the risotto, allowing the rice to absorb the liquid before adding more. Keep the heat under the risotto on low–medium and keep stirring all the time with a wooden spoon, to avoid the rice sticking to the bottom of the pan. Once cooked, remove from the heat and beat in butter and Parmesan, if appropriate to the recipe, to give the risotto that extra creaminess.

RISOTTO CAPRESE

RISOTTO WITH TOMATO, MOZZARELLA, AND BASIL

The ingredients for this risotto are taken from the classic *Caprese* salad—tomatoes, mozzarella, and basil. Simple to make and extremely tasty, it's often my go-to midweek meal for the family.

Cooking time: 30 minutes

Serves 4

3 tbsp/1½ oz/40 g butter
2 tbsp extra-virgin olive oil
1 small onion, finely chopped
2 handfuls of basil leaves
1¾ cups/9¼ oz/260 g cherry tomatoes,
    quartered
1¾ cups/11¼ oz/320 g risotto rice,
    such as Arborio
scant ½ cup/100 ml white wine
6½ cups/1.5 liters hot vegetable stock
7 oz/200 g mozzarella, cut into small cubes
⅓ cup/1 oz/30 g grated Parmesan

Heat 1½ tablespoons/¾ oz/20 g of the butter and the olive oil in a large, heavy-based saucepan set over medium heat. Add the onion and a couple of the basil leaves and sweat for 2 minutes. Stir in the tomatoes and continue to sweat for 1 minute. Stir in the rice, making sure each grain is coated in oil. Add the wine and cook until the rice has absorbed it. Then add a couple of ladles of hot stock, stirring with a wooden spoon until the rice has absorbed it all. Add a couple more ladles of stock and continue to cook in this way, stirring and adding more stock, for 17–20 minutes, until the risotto is cooked *al dente*.

Remove from the heat, add the remaining butter and mozzarella, and stir well until it has nicely melted into the risotto. Stir in the grated Parmesan and remaining basil leaves and serve immediately.

RISOTTO FESTIVO

CELEBRATION RISOTTO WITH PROSECCO, SHRIMP, AND SCALLOPS

The perfect risotto for a special occasion! After you've added the prosecco into the risotto, have some glasses at the ready and share it among your guests. It's such an easy dish to make that you too can afford to indulge in a glass while cooking! When adding the butter at the end, known in Italian as *mantecare* ("to cook until creamy"), be careful not to mix too vigorously, to avoid the seafood breaking up. It won't affect the flavor, but it does look prettier to have the seafood whole when serving.

Cooking time: 30 minutes

Serves 4

3 tbsp/1½ oz/40 g butter,
   plus an extra pat to serve
2 tbsp extra-virgin olive oil,
   plus extra for drizzling
2 shallots, finely chopped
1¾ cups/11¼ oz/320 g risotto rice,
   such as Arborio
½ cup/120 ml prosecco
5½ cups/1.3 liters hot vegetable stock
12 scallops
12 jumbo shrimp
a handful of fresh parsley, finely chopped

Heat the butter and olive oil in a large saucepan set over medium heat. Add the shallots and sweat for 1 minute. Stir in the rice, making sure each grain is coated in oil. Add the prosecco, increase the heat, and allow the alcohol to evaporate. Then add a couple of ladles of hot stock, stirring with a wooden spoon until the rice has absorbed it all. Add a couple more ladles of stock and continue to cook in this way, stirring and adding more stock, for 17–20 minutes, until the risotto is cooked *al dente*. About 5 minutes before the end of the cooking time, stir in the scallops and shrimp. Remove from the heat, mix in the extra pat of butter and the parsley, and serve with a drizzle of extra-virgin olive oil.

RISOTTO AI CALAMARI E ZAFFERANO

CALAMARI AND SAFFRON RISOTTO

This risotto makes a lovely meal at any time and the saffron gives it a nice yellow color. The addition of lightly toasted pine nuts gives the dish a nice crunch, contrasting with the soft calamari. I like to add a pinch of red pepper flakes to mine, to give it an extra kick!

Cooking time: 25–30 minutes (not including prep)

Serves 4

¼ cup/60 ml extra-virgin olive oil,
    plus extra for drizzling
2 small shallots, finely chopped
14 oz/400 g squid, sliced into rings
1¾ cups/11¼ oz/320 g risotto rice,
    such as Arborio
⅔ cup/150 ml white wine
6½ cups/1.5 liters hot vegetable stock
a few saffron strands, diluted in a little of the
    vegetable stock
2 tbsp/1 oz/30 g butter
a handful of fresh parsley, finely chopped
⅓ cup/1¾ oz/50 g pine nuts (optional)
2 tsp dried red pepper flakes (optional)

Heat the olive oil in a large, heavy-based saucepan over high heat, add the shallots, and sweat for 1 minute, then add the calamari and fry, stirring, for 4 minutes. Stir in the rice, making sure each grain is coated in oil. Add the wine and cook until the rice has absorbed it. Reduce the heat to medium and add a couple of ladles of hot stock, stirring with a wooden spoon until the rice has absorbed it all. Add a couple more ladles of stock and continue to cook in this way, stirring and adding more stock, for about 20 minutes, until the rice is *al dente*.

Remove from the heat, add the diluted saffron strands, butter, and parsley, and mix well.

Heat a small frying pan, add the pine nuts, and cook for 1 minute or so until toasted.

Divide the risotto among 4 bowls, top with the toasted pine nuts and chili flakes, if desired, and add a final drizzle of extra-virgin olive oil to serve.

RISOTTO AL ZAFFERANO CON PORCINI SECCHI

SAFFRON RISOTTO WITH DRIED PORCINI

This traditional Milanese classic, with the addition of dried porcini mushrooms, is delicious and a must for any mushroom lover. In season, you could make this dish with fresh porcini, but dried are so easily obtainable from Italian delis and supermarkets that I always keep a packet in my store cupboard.

Cooking time: 35 minutes

Serves 4

⅓ cup/1¾ oz/50 g dried porcini mushrooms
a couple of saffron strands
1 small onion
2½ tbsp/1¼ oz/35 g butter
2 tbsp extra-virgin olive oil
1¾ cups/11¼ oz/320 g risotto rice,
   such as Arborio
scant ½ cup/100 ml white wine
6½ cups/1.5 liters hot vegetable stock
¾ cup/1¾ oz/50 g grated Parmesan, plus extra
   for serving

Soak the dried porcini and saffron strands in a little warm water and set aside for about 10 minutes, for the porcini to soften.

Meanwhile, finely chop the onion and prepare the other ingredients.

Heat half of the butter and the olive oil in a medium, heavy-based saucepan set over medium heat. Add the onion and sweat for a couple of minutes. Stir in the softened porcini (keeping the soaking liquid) and fry, stirring, for 1 minute. Stir in the rice, making sure each grain is coated in oil. Add the white wine and the reserved porcini soaking liquid and cook, stirring with a wooden spoon, until the liquid has been absorbed by the rice. Add a couple of ladles of hot stock and cook, continuously stirring, until absorbed. Continue adding stock and cooking in this way for 17–20 minutes, until the risotto is cooked *al dente*.

Remove from the heat, mix in the remaining butter and the grated Parmesan, and serve immediately, with an extra grating of Parmesan, if desired.

RISOTTO DI CAROTA E SEDANO RAPA
CARROT AND CELERIAC RISOTTO

Carrot and celeriac (celery root) is a match made in heaven and is one of my partner Liz's favorite food combinations. In fact, she came up with this idea for a risotto when we had some leftover celeriac and we have been making it ever since—we now purposely buy celeriac to make this dish! Grating the vegetables not only makes them quick to cook, but helps them mush nicely into the risotto. This makes a perfect one-pot meal for a mid-week family supper.

Cooking time: 30 minutes (not including vegetable prep)

Serves 4

3½ tbsp/1¾ oz/50 g butter
3 tbsp extra-virgin olive oil
1 small onion, finely chopped
2 carrots, peeled and grated
2 cups/7 oz/200 g peeled and grated celeriac
    (celery root)
scant 2 cups/11¾ oz/340 g risotto rice,
    such as Arborio
scant ½ cup/100 ml white wine
6½ cups/1.5 liters hot vegetable stock
generous ½ cup/1½ oz/40 g grated Parmesan,
    plus extra for serving
a handful of parsley, finely chopped

Heat 2 tablespoons/1 oz/30 g of the butter and the olive oil in a large, heavy-based saucepan set over medium heat. Add the onion, carrots, and celeriac and sweat for 4–5 minutes. Stir in the rice, making sure each grain is coated in oil. Add the wine and cook until the rice has absorbed it. Then add a couple of ladles of hot stock, stirring with a wooden spoon until the rice has absorbed it all. Add a couple more ladles of stock and continue to cook in this way, stirring and adding more stock, for 17–20 minutes, until the risotto is cooked *al dente*.

Remove from the heat, add the remaining butter and Parmesan, and mix well with a wooden spoon. Stir in the parsley and serve immediately, with an extra sprinkling of Parmesan, if desired.

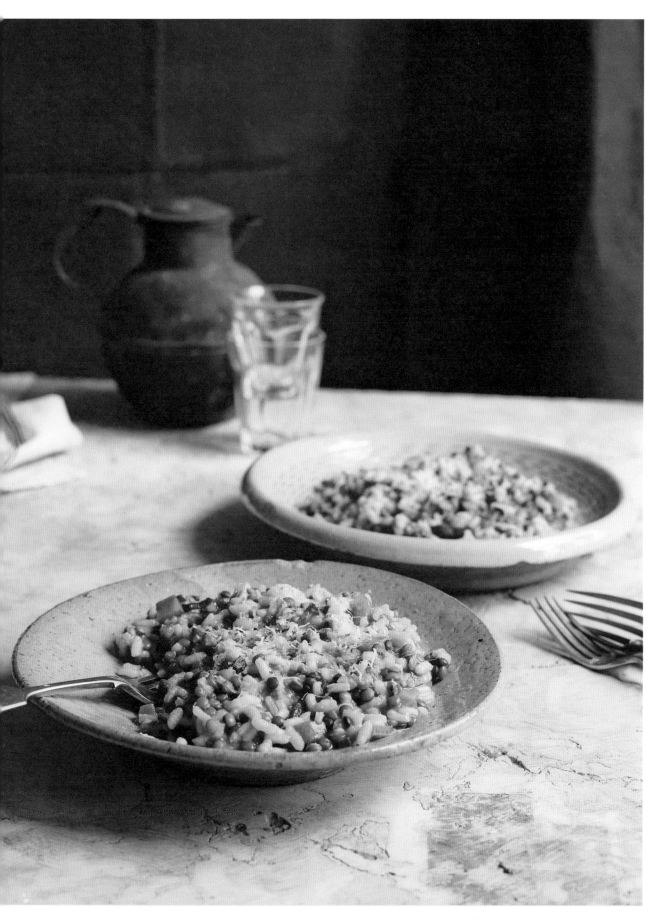

RISOTTO CON LENTICCHIE
LENTIL RISOTTO

This is a super, nutritious one-pot meal. Try to get Castelluccio lentils from Umbria, which should be available from good Italian delis. Not only do they cook quickly, but they taste delicious. If you can't get them, then use small brown or green lentils that don't require pre-soaking. If you are really pressed for time, use good-quality organic canned lentils, which, once drained, you can add about halfway through making the risotto.

Cooking time: 30–35 minutes

Serves 4–6

1½ cups/9 oz/250 g Castelluccio lentils
3 tbsp/1½ oz/40 g butter
1 tbsp extra-virgin olive oil
3½ oz/100 g pancetta, finely chopped
1 garlic clove, left whole
1 rosemary sprig
1 celery stalk, finely chopped
1 carrot, finely chopped
scant ½ cup/3½ oz/100 g canned
    chopped tomatoes
1⅓ cups/9 oz/250 g risotto rice,
    such as Arborio
6½ cups/1.5 liters hot vegetable stock
⅓ cup/1 oz/30 g grated Parmesan,
    plus extra for serving

Place the lentils in a saucepan, cover with water, bring to a boil, and simmer for 10 minutes.

Meanwhile, heat 1½ tablespoons/¾ oz/20 g of the butter and the olive oil in a large, heavy-based saucepan set over high heat. Add the pancetta and sauté for 2 minutes, then reduce the heat to medium, add the garlic, rosemary, celery, and carrot and sweat for 4 minutes. Stir in the tomatoes and cook for about 3 minutes.

By this time the lentils should be cooked. Drain the lentils and add to the mixture in the pan. Stir in the rice, making sure each grain is coated in oil. Add a couple of ladles of hot stock, stirring with a wooden spoon until the rice has absorbed it all. Add a couple more ladles of stock and continue to cook in this way, stirring and adding more stock, for 17–20 minutes, until the rice is *al dente* and the lentils are cooked.

Remove from the heat, discard the garlic, if you like, then stir in the remaining butter and Parmesan. Serve immediately with extra grated Parmesan, if desired.

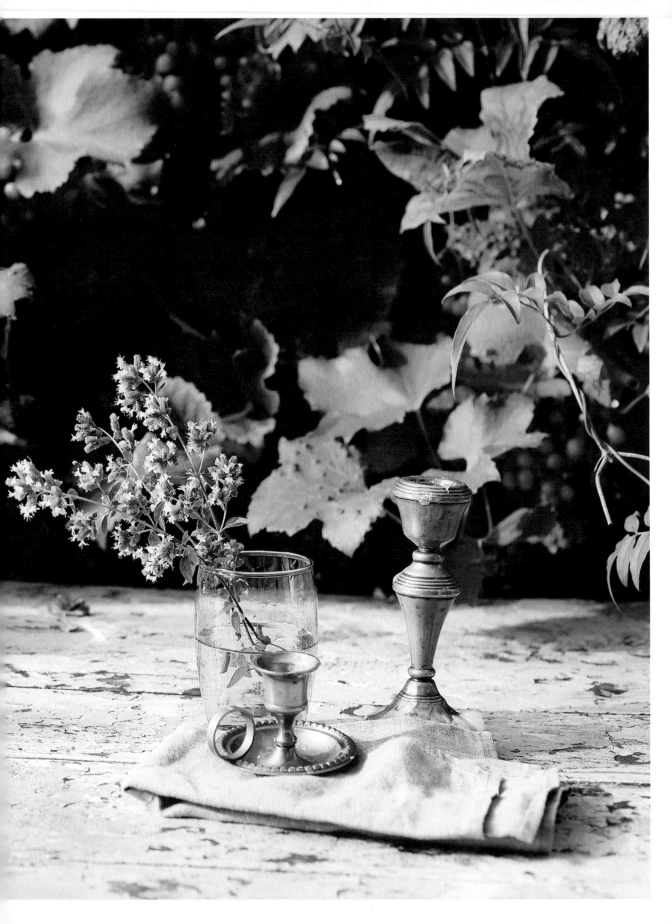

RISOTTO CON VONGOLE E PEPERONI MISTI

RISOTTO WITH CLAMS AND MIXED PEPPERS

For this recipe, I urge you to get the freshest and best clams you can; the liquid exuded from them gives the risotto its rich, delicious flavor. For speed, you can buy pre-sliced mixed peppers. The resulting dish is a colorful feast for the eyes and treat for the palate. A lovely dish to serve for a relaxed supper with friends, it is perfectly accompanied by a cold, crisp white wine such as a Greco di Tufo from Campania, or a Lugana from Lake Garda.

Cooking time: 35 minutes

Serves 4

2 lb 4 oz/1 kg clams
1¼ cups/300 ml white wine
1 garlic clove, left whole
a handful of parsley, finely chopped,
    with a few sprigs reserved whole
¼ cup/60 ml extra-virgin olive oil,
    plus extra for drizzling
2 banana shallots, finely chopped
14 oz/400 g mixed green, red, and yellow
    bell peppers, thinly sliced
scant 2 cups/11¾ oz/340 g risotto rice,
    such as Arborio
2½ cups/600 ml hot vegetable stock

Place the clams, half of the white wine, the garlic, and a few whole sprigs of parsley into a large, heavy-based saucepan. Cover with a lid and cook over medium heat for 2–3 minutes, until the clam shells have opened.

Meanwhile, heat the olive oil in another large saucepan set over medium heat, add the shallots, and sweat for a couple of minutes. Increase the heat, add the peppers, and fry, stirring, for 3 minutes.

Drain the clams, reserving the cooking liquid, and set both aside. Discard any clams that have not opened.

Stir the rice into the pan with the peppers, making sure each grain is coated with oil. Add the remaining white wine and cook until it is absorbed. Add the liquid from the clams, reduce the heat to medium, and cook, stirring with a wooden spoon, until it has been absorbed. Add a couple of ladles of hot stock, stirring with a wooden spoon until the rice has absorbed it. Add a couple more ladles of stock and continue to cook in this way, stirring and adding more stock, for 17–20 minutes, until the rice is *al dente*.

At the end of the cooking time, stir in the clams. Serve immediately, with the finely chopped parsley and a drizzle of extra-virgin olive oil.

RISOTTO AI QUATTRO FORMAGGI
RISOTTO WITH 4 CHEESES

This has to be one of my favorite comfort foods. It's an ideal recipe to make when you have lots of pieces of leftover cheese in the refrigerator. The cheeses I have used are all typically Italian, but you can of course use whatever you have on hand—I find Cheddar is always such a good choice.

Cooking time: 25–30 minutes

Serves 4

3½ tbsp/1¾ oz/50 g butter
2 tbsp extra-virgin olive oil
1 small onion, finely chopped
2 cups/12 oz/350 g risotto rice, such as
    Arborio
scant ½ cup/100 ml white wine
6½ cups/1.5 liters hot vegetable stock
1¾ oz/50 g Taleggio, roughly cut into small
    cubes
1¾ oz/50 g Dolcelatte, roughly cut into small
    cubes
¾ cup/1¾ oz/50 g grated Pecorino
¾ cup/1¾ oz/50 g grated Parmesan
a handful of fresh parsley, finely chopped
    (optional)

Heat 2 tablespoons/1 oz/30 g of the butter and the olive oil in a medium, heavy-based saucepan set over medium heat. Add the onion and sweat for a couple of minutes. Stir in the rice, making sure each grain is coated in oil. Add the wine and cook until the rice has absorbed it. Then add a couple of ladles of hot stock, stirring with a wooden spoon, until the rice has absorbed it all. Add more stock and continue to cook in this way for 17–20 minutes, until the risotto is cooked *al dente*.

Remove from the heat, add the remaining butter and all of the cheeses, and mix well until the Taleggio and Dolcelatte have nicely melted. Serve immediately, with a little chopped parsley, if desired.

RISOTTO CON SALSICCIA

SAUSAGE RISOTTO

This simple risotto makes a fantastic mid-week meal for the whole family to enjoy. Ensure you get good-quality Italian pork sausages, available from good Italian delis. My favorite ones are the fennel-infused variety, but for a milder flavor go for *luganica* (a long, narrow sausage from northern Italy), or ask your deli to see what they have.

Cooking time: 30 minutes (not including prep)

Serves 4

3 tbsp/1½ oz/40 g butter
2 tbsp extra-virgin olive oil
1 small red onion, finely chopped
2 rosemary sprigs, needles only
10½ oz/300 g Italian pork sausages, skins
    removed and meat crumbled
1¾ cups/11½ oz/325 g risotto rice, such as
    Arborio
scant ½ cup/100 ml white wine
6½ cups/1.5 liters hot vegetable stock
generous ½ cup/1½ oz/40 g grated Parmesan

Heat half of the butter and the olive oil in a large saucepan set over medium heat. Add the onion and sweat for a minute or so, until softened. Add the rosemary and sausage meat, increase the heat to high, and fry, stirring, for 3–4 minutes, until seared. Stir in the rice, making sure each grain is coated in oil. Add the wine and cook until the rice has absorbed it. Reduce the heat to medium, and add a couple of ladles of hot stock, stirring with a wooden spoon until the rice has absorbed it all. Add a couple more ladles of stock and continue to cook in this way, stirring and adding more stock, for 17–20 minutes, until the rice is *al dente*.

Remove from the heat, add the remaining butter and the Parmesan, mix well, and serve right away.

FISH

Fish is extremely quick and easy to cook and really doesn't need too many ingredients or fancy ways of cooking. For me, the best fish is simply grilled or steamed and served with a drizzle of good extra-virgin olive oil and a squeeze of lemon. This is how most Italians enjoy fish, and as long as the fish is fresh, you can't go wrong.

I was lucky to have been born by the sea, where fresh fish was readily available, so it was not uncommon for us to eat it quite a few times a week. Since we knew most of the fishermen in the area, I was often allowed to go with them and help out and, in return, they would give me local seafood to take home.

I love the markets in Italy with their fabulous displays of fresh fish. Whenever I'm home, I make sure I buy fresh anchovies and make *acciughe alla tortiera*, a very simple baked dish. I also preserve fresh anchovies in salt so that I can bring them home to enjoy the taste of the sea all year round.

Fish is highly nutritious, low in fat, and an excellent source of quality protein, vitamins, and minerals. Scientific evidence suggests that eating fish a couple of times a week helps preserve mental agility and aids longevity. I remember my mother would make me eat fish eyes, which, when cooked, became little white, hard balls full of phosphorus. She said it was a nutrient that helped develop intelligence!

It's sad that a lot of neighborhood fishmongers have closed in recent times. However, fish counters in supermarkets are now becoming increasingly adventurous, with monkfish, skate wings, gurnard, squid, fresh tuna, and more, making regular appearances alongside salmon and cod.

TONNO FRESCO CON VERDURE IN OLIO

FRESH TUNA WITH PRESERVED VEGETABLES

This is a perfect meal for a warm summer's evening. Fresh tuna is almost meat-like in texture, but still incredibly light. Good-quality preserved grilled vegetables are obtainable from your Italian deli counter. The crunch of the red onion perfectly complements this dish.

Cooking time: 10 minutes

Serves 4

scant 1 cup/5¾ oz/160 g preserved
   grilled zucchini
scant 1 cup/5¾ oz/160 g preserved
   grilled eggplants
1 small red onion, finely sliced
3 cups/2 oz/60 g arugula
⅔ cup/4¼ oz/120 g baby plum
   tomatoes, sliced
12 basil leaves (optional)
¼ cup/60 ml extra-virgin olive oil, plus an
   extra splash for cooking
1 lb/450 g fresh tuna, cut into chunks
¼ cup/1 oz/30 g pine nuts
2 tbsp balsamic vinegar
sea salt and freshly ground black pepper

Arrange the preserved vegetables, red onion, arugula, tomatoes, and basil leaves, if using, on a large serving dish.

Heat a griddle, or place a frying pan over medium heat with a splash of extra-virgin olive oil. Add the tuna chunks and cook for a couple of minutes on each side, until seared.

Top the vegetables on the serving platter with the seared tuna, sprinkle with pine nuts, drizzle with the extra-virgin olive oil and balsamic vinegar, and season with some salt and pepper. Mix together well and serve.

SGOMBRI AL CARTOCCIO AL PROFUMO DI LIMONE

LEMON-INFUSED STEAM-BAKED MACKEREL

I love mackerel—not only is it a lovely fish, but it's nutritious and quick to cook. Cooking *al cartoccio* is an excellent way of keeping all the flavors intact in a healthy way. Serve the cooked mackerel in the foil, so that the delicious juices can be enjoyed with some good bread to mop them up.

Cooking time: 30 minutes (including prep)

Serves 2

2 mackerel (about 8½ oz/240 g each), heads
    removed (if desired) and cleaned
sea salt and freshly ground black pepper
2 rosemary sprigs
1 garlic clove, finely chopped
2 organic unwaxed lemons, finely sliced
extra-virgin olive oil

Preheat the oven to 400°F/200°C.

Rinse the mackerel under cold running water, then pat dry well with paper towels. Place the fish on a large piece of parchment paper, which is in turn placed on top of a large piece of good-quality aluminium foil (you can place the fish on individual sheets or all in one package, as here). Place on a baking tray. Sprinkle salt and pepper all over the mackerel, including inside the cavity. Place a rosemary sprig inside each cavity, together with the garlic and half of the lemon slices. Top the mackerel with the remaining lemon slices, drizzle with olive oil, then wrap tightly in the foil and bake in the hot oven for 20 minutes.

To serve, place the whole parcel in the middle of the table and dig in!

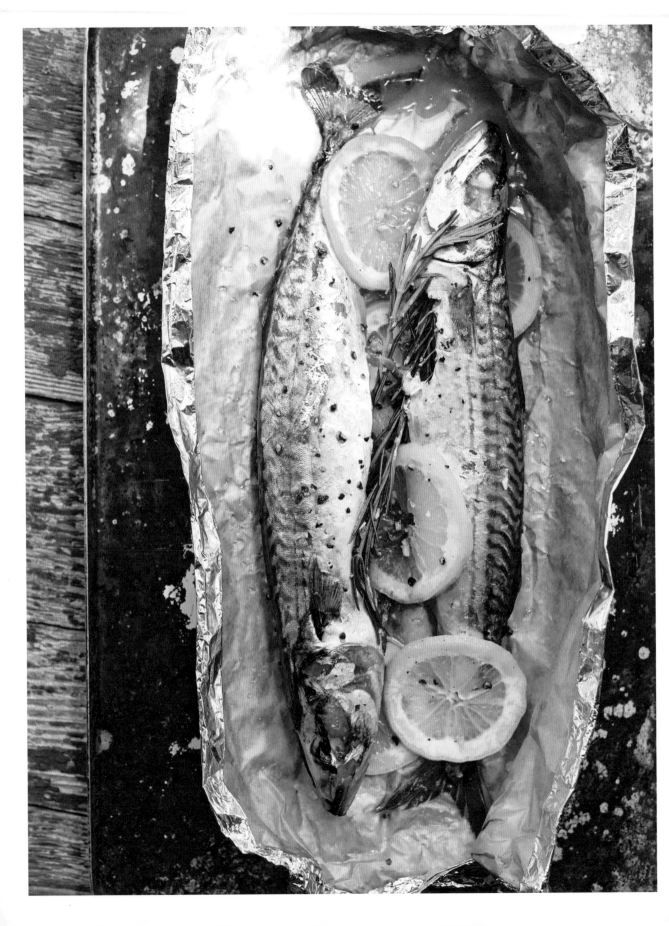

MERLUZZO CON PATATE ASSORTITE E AGRODOLCE DI CIPOLLA ROSSA

HAKE WITH MIXED POTATOES AND RED ONION AGRODOLCE

This lovely, delicate fish dish, enhanced by a selection of colored potatoes and slight tangy onion *agrodolce*, makes a perfect main course when you're trying to impress! Chunks of hake are gently cooked with herbs and good extra-virgin olive oil, while a trio of potatoes are baking in the oven. Not only is it an attractive, vibrant dish, but both purple and sweet potatoes are highly nutritious with many health benefits.

Cooking time: 35–40 minutes (including prep)

Serves 4

1 lb 12 oz/780 g mixture of purple potatoes, sweet potatoes, and white potatoes
16 sage leaves
2 bay leaves
sea salt
6 tbsp/90 ml extra-virgin olive oil, plus extra for drizzling
2 rosemary sprigs
1 tsp pink peppercorns
14 oz/400 g hake, cut into 4 chunks
½ red onion, very finely sliced
1 tsp capers
2 tsp white wine vinegar

Preheat the oven to 425°F/220°C.

Wash the potatoes, dry them, then cut into halves or quarters depending on their size (keep the skins on). Add the chunks to a large saucepan filled with water and parboil for 10 minutes. Drain well, place in a roasting dish with 8 sage leaves and the bay leaves, sprinkle with some salt, and drizzle with a little olive oil. Bake in the hot oven for about 15–20 minutes, until cooked through and beginning to color.

Meanwhile, in a pan large enough to fit the fish chunks, add the olive oil, the remaining sage, rosemary, and pink peppercorns, and cook over low heat for a minute or so, to allow the herbs to infuse. When the olive oil begins to bubble slightly, add the hake chunks, cover with a lid, and continue to cook over low heat for 15 minutes, carefully turning the fish over halfway through.

Meanwhile, to make the *agrodolce*, combine the red onion, capers, and white wine vinegar in a small dish.

Arrange the potatoes and fish on a large serving dish. Alternatively, divide among plates, making sure everyone gets a selection of colored potatoes. Drizzle the herby cooking juices from the pan over the top, followed by the onion *agrodolce*.

SOGLIOLA CON SPECK E CIPOLLOTTI

FILLETS OF SOLE WITH SPECK AND CIPOLLOTTI ONIONS

Sole is a light, delicate fish that marries really well with the slight smoky aroma of speck, a cured ham from north-east Italy. Speck is obtainable from good Italian delis, but if you prefer, you could substitute the slightly blander-tasting prosciutto. *Cipollotti*, sometimes called spring onions, are a large version of scallions, which you can get in farmers markets; otherwise, buy the largest scallions you can find or substitute with shallots or leeks. A quick and simple dish, this makes a lovely and impressive main course, especially when you have guests over.

Cooking time: 25–30 minutes (including prep)

Serves 2–4

9 oz/250 g skinless sole fillets
sea salt and freshly ground black pepper
4 slices of speck
1½ tbsp/¾ oz/20 g butter
2 tbsp extra-virgin olive oil
5½ oz/150 g *cipollotti* onions, trimmed and
    sliced in half
⅓ cup/80 ml white wine

Slice the sole fillets in half lengthways and season lightly all over with salt and pepper. Lay the speck slices on a board, place a sole fillet on top of each, and roll up. Set aside.

In a large frying pan set over high heat, melt the butter and 1 tablespoon of the olive oil, add the *cipollotti*, and sweat for 1 minute. Add 3 tablespoons of the wine, cover with a lid, reduce the heat to medium, and cook for 4–5 minutes, until the *cipollotti* are just tender. Remove the *cipollotti* from the pan and keep warm.

Place the remaining olive oil in the pan, add the wrapped sole fillets, cover with a lid, and cook over medium heat for 10 minutes, carefully turning them over halfway through. Increase the heat, add the remaining wine, and allow to cook off. Remove from the heat and serve immediately with the *cipollotti*.

FILETTI DI TROTA ALLA VENDEMIA

BAKED TROUT AND GRAPES WITH A RED WINE SAUCE

The Italian title of this dish suggests harvest time and a dish such as this would be cooked in rural wine-making areas using meat rather than fish. However, I find earthy-tasting fillets of trout work just as well and the combination of slightly crunchy vegetables, soft sweet-tasting grapes, and the slightly bitter wine sauce go really well together. Don't worry if you find the wine sauce too bitter on tasting—eating it together with the fish will change your mind!

Cooking time: 30 minutes (not including vegetable prep)

Serves 4

4 trout fillets (about 5½ oz/150 g each)
sea salt and freshly ground black pepper
3½ tbsp/1¾ oz/50 g butter
1 onion, thinly sliced
2 celery stalks, thinly sliced
1 large carrot, sliced into thin batons
2 bay leaves
2 thyme sprigs
1⅓ cups/7 oz/200 g green grapes
1⅓ cups/7 oz/200 g red grapes
¼ cup/1 oz/30 g pine nuts
2½ tbsp all-purpose flour
1¼ cups/300 ml red wine

Preheat the oven to 350°F/180°C.

Place the trout fillets in a baking dish and season with a little salt and pepper.

Melt 2 tablespoons/1 oz/30 g of the butter in a frying pan set over medium heat. Add the vegetables, herbs, and grapes and sweat for 3 minutes. Pour this over the fish, sprinkle with pine nuts, cover with foil, and cook in the hot oven for 20 minutes.

Meanwhile, prepare the sauce. Melt the remaining 1½ tablespoons/¾ oz/20 g butter in a small saucepan set over medium heat. Remove from the heat and whisk in the flour, mixing well to avoid lumps. Add a couple of tablespoons of the red wine and continue to whisk. Place back over the heat, gradually add all the wine, whisking all the time, and cook until the sauce has thickened.

Remove the fish from the oven, carefully divide among the plates, and serve with the wine sauce.

BRANZINO CON FUNGHI
SEABASS WITH FORESTIERE MUSHROOMS

When I originally set out to make this recipe, I wanted to use porcini mushrooms; however, I was testing out of season and porcini were unavailable. I found a type of cultivated mushroom called *Forestiere,* which looks similar to large, brown cremini mushroom. The mushroom has a slightly wild, forest-y taste and works really well with the seabass. If you can't find this type, any cultivated brown or white mushroom is fine, and, of course, if you can get porcini during the fall, then this quick, simple dish will be a real treat! Serve with some boiled baby potatoes for a delicious meal.

Cooking time: 15 minutes (not including prep)

Serves 4

3 tbsp extra-virgin olive oil,
    plus an extra splash
2 garlic cloves, finely chopped
5½ oz/150 g *Forestiere* mushrooms,
    thinly sliced
sea salt and freshly ground black pepper
1⅔ cups/8½ oz/240 g cherry tomatoes, halved
a handful of fresh parsley, coarsely chopped
2 tbsp/1 oz/30 g butter
4 seabass fillets (about 4½ oz/125 g each)

Heat the olive oil in a frying pan, add the garlic, and sweat over medium heat for 1 minute. Add the mushrooms, season with some salt and pepper, and fry, stirring, for 1 minute. Remove the mushrooms and set aside.

In the same pan, add the tomatoes with another splash of olive oil, and fry, stirring, for 2 minutes. Return the mushrooms to the pan and continue to cook for a further 2 minutes. Stir in the parsley and turn off the heat.

Meanwhile, in another, larger frying pan, melt the butter, add the fish, skin-side down, season with some salt and pepper, and fry over medium heat for 5 minutes. Turn the fish over carefully and cook for a further 2 minutes, until cooked through.

Serve the fish with the mushroom mixture.

FILETTI DI PLATESSA CON BURRO, LIMONE E CAPPERI

PLAICE FILLETS WITH BUTTER, LEMON, AND CAPERS, SERVED WITH BABY POTATOES

I had never tasted flatfish until I came to England and found plaice on menus at fish and chip shops. In Italy, anchovies and capers are often added to fish dishes, so I wanted to combine these Italian ingredients with the flavorful flatfish, plaice. If you can't source plaice, lemon sole works just as well. The combination of capers and lemon juice is a winner and gives a delicious kick to the dish. Be careful not to add too much salt to the fish, because anchovies and capers are quite salty. Served with minty, boiled baby potatoes, this makes a lovely light and nutritious meal, perfect for a quick and easy mid-week supper, as well as for entertaining. I love to mop up the buttery lemon sauce with some good bread at the end!

Cooking time: 15–20 minutes (including prep)

Serves 2–4

1 lb 2 oz/500 g baby potatoes, scrubbed
4 plaice or lemon sole fillets
    (about 6¼ oz/180 g each)
sea salt
6 tbsp/3 oz/90 g butter, plus an extra pat
2 anchovy fillets, finely chopped
2 tbsp capers in brine (if under salt, ensure
    you wash salt off completely)
juice of 1 large organic unwaxed lemon
1 tbsp chopped fresh parsley
a handful of fresh mint, finely chopped

Place the baby potatoes in a large saucepan of water, bring to a boil, and cook for about 10 minutes, until the potatoes are tender.

Meanwhile, season the fish with very little salt. Heat 2 tablespoons/1 oz/30 g of the butter in a large frying pan set over medium heat. Add the anchovy fillets and sauté for a couple of minutes until the anchovies dissolve. Holding the plaice fillets with your fingertips, dip both sides into the buttery mixture, before placing each fillet skin-side down into the pan. Add the capers, half of the lemon juice, an additional 2 tablespoons/1 oz/30 g of the butter, and the parsley, and cook for 2–3 minutes, until the fish is cooked through. Remove the fish to a serving dish and set aside. Increase the heat, add 1 tablespoon/½ oz/15 g butter to the pan, stirring well until melted, then remove from the heat and pour over the fish, together with the remaining lemon juice.

Drain the potatoes, toss with the remaining 1 tablespoon/½ oz/15 g butter and the mint, and serve immediately with the fish.

CALAMARI ALLE OLIVE

CALAMARI WITH OLIVES

This is a traditional southern Italian dish that is perfect to enjoy with a group of friends for a casual supper. Serve with lots of toasted rustic bread to mop up the tomato sauce.

Cooking time: 25 minutes

Serves 4–6

2 lb 4 oz/1 kg cleaned squid
¼ cup/60 ml extra-virgin olive oil
2 banana shallots, finely chopped
2 garlic cloves, finely chopped
a handful of fresh parsley, finely chopped
sea salt and freshly ground black pepper
scant ½ cup/100 ml white wine
1 cup/8½ oz/240 g tomato passata or purée
2 cups/7 oz/200 g black olives
toasted rustic bread, to serve

Wash the squid under cold running water, pat dry on paper towels, and cut into rings.

Heat the olive oil in a large saucepan set over medium heat. Add the shallots, garlic, and parsley and sweat for a couple of minutes. Stir in the squid rings, season with a little salt and pepper, increase the heat to high, and fry, stirring, for 1 minute. Add the white wine and allow the alcohol to cook off for a minute or so. Add the tomato passata and olives, cover with a lid, reduce the heat to medium, and cook for 15 minutes. Serve immediately, with the bread on the side.

SALMONE CON FINOCCHIO

SALMON WITH FENNEL

Salmon and fennel go well together, and the addition of the creamy sauce makes this a very tasty meal that can be made in no time. Since the salmon is coated in flour and fried, it retains a slight crispiness on the outside, which combines perfectly with the slightly crunchy fennel.

Cooking time: 30 minutes (including prep)

Serves 4

2 fennel bulbs
zest and juice of 1 lemon
4 salmon fillets (about 4 oz/115 g each)
sea salt and freshly ground black pepper
all-purpose flour, for coating
5½ tbsp/2¾ oz/80 g butter
a splash of white wine
scant ½ cup/100 ml heavy whipping cream
⅓ cup/1 oz/30 g grated Parmesan

Preheat the oven to 425°F/220°C.

Remove the green fronds from the fennel bulb and set aside. Slice each bulb into 8 segments, place into acidulated water (water mixed with the lemon juice), and set aside.

Cut each salmon fillet into 4 chunks, sprinkle with salt and pepper, and coat in flour. Heat 3 tablespoons/1½ oz/40 g of the butter in a frying pan set over medium heat. Add the salmon chunks and sear on both sides, for about 3–4 minutes. Add a splash of white wine and cook for a further minute. Remove the salmon and set aside.

In the same pan, heat the remaining butter, add the fennel segments and some salt and pepper, and cook on medium–high heat for a couple of minutes on both sides.

Combine the cream, Parmesan, and lemon zest and season with some more salt and pepper.

Arrange the fennel in a baking dish, place the salmon chunks on top and pour over the creamy mixture. Bake in the hot oven for 5 minutes, until golden. Serve, sprinkled with the reserved fennel fronds.

PESCATRICE IN PADELLA CON SALSA DI ALLORO

PAN-FRIED MONKFISH WITH A BAY LEAF AND SHALLOT SAUCE

This dish is quick and simple to prepare; while the monkfish is cooking, you can get on with making the sauce at the same time. I like to serve this dish with lots of good crusty bread to mop up the sauce. Make sure you use a good-quality dry, crisp white wine, otherwise you could get a bitter aftertaste. If you prefer, you can substitute the monkfish with cod or hake.

Cooking time: 20 minutes

Serves 2–4

2 monkfish tails (about 1 lb 7 oz/650 g in total)
sea salt and freshly ground black pepper
⅓ cup/80 ml extra-virgin olive oil
3 anchovy fillets

For the sauce:
1 tsp cornstarch
1½ cups/350 ml white wine
½ cup/120 ml extra-virgin olive oil
8 bay leaves, finely chopped
2 shallots, finely chopped
2 garlic cloves, finely chopped
a handful of parsley, finely chopped

Cut each monkfish tail in half, so that you have 4 pieces of fish, and season with a little salt and pepper.

Heat the olive oil in a frying pan set over medium heat. Add the anchovies and cook until dissolved. Add the monkfish and cook for 5 minutes on each side.

Meanwhile, make the sauce: blend the cornstarch with the white wine and set aside. In a small saucepan set over medium heat, heat the olive oil, add the bay leaves, shallots, and garlic and sweat for about 4 minutes. Stir in the parsley, add the white wine mixture, increase the heat, and cook for 5–6 minutes, until the sauce thickens. Remove from the heat, season with salt and pepper, and serve with the monkfish.

RAZZA CON POMODORINI, AGLIO E BASILICO

SKATE WITH CHERRY TOMATOES, GARLIC, AND BASIL

I love skate—whenever I see it at the fishmonger I have to buy it and usually cook it in this simple, very southern-Italian way. Served with slices of toasted country bread, it makes a substantial meal for two, although if you are serving other food, you could stretch it to three servings. You can serve the sauce with linguine or spaghetti as an appetizer and enjoy the fish as a main course—this is quite common in Italy. If you do this, add the cooked pasta at the end when the sauce is reducing.

Cooking time: 20 minutes (including prep)

Serves 2

1 large skate wing (about 1 lb 2 oz/500 g)
sea salt and freshly ground black pepper
6 tbsp/90 ml extra-virgin olive oil
4 garlic cloves, finely sliced
¼ fresh red chili pepper, finely chopped
2 tsp capers
14 oz/400 g baby plum tomatoes, halved
1 cup/250 ml freshly boiled water
2 tbsp white wine
a handful of basil leaves
2–4 slices of sourdough bread, toasted

Season the skate all over with salt and pepper.

In a frying pan large enough to accommodate the skate (if necessary, slice the fish to fit the pan), heat the olive oil over medium heat. Add the garlic, chili pepper, and capers and sweat for about 30 seconds, then add the tomatoes and cook for a further 30 seconds. Add the hot water, wine, basil, and some salt and cook for 3 minutes. Add the skate, cover the pan, and cook for 10–12 minutes, carefully turning the skate over halfway through, until the fish is cooked.

Carefully remove the fish from the pan and place on a serving dish. Increase the heat to high and cook the tomato sauce for a couple of minutes, until it has reduced slightly. Remove from the heat, pour the sauce over the fish, and serve with slices of toasted sourdough bread.

MEAT

When it comes to meat, one of my guilty pleasures is a nice, juicy, medium-rare steak *ai ferri,* which means grilled without adding any fat. Quick and simple to prepare, it takes no time to cook and, together with a mixed salad and some bread, it is a feast for a king!

When buying meat that requires little cooking time, I cannot stress enough the importance of getting the best, organic, ethically sourced meat you can afford. Good-quality meat is an excellent source of protein, but you don't have to eat it every day. I find I am going back to my childhood days when we really only had meat on Sundays and feast days, but it was always good-quality and more often than not we knew the farmer. So not only did we know where our meat came from, but it was always full of flavor and needed little seasoning.

In Italy, a small piece of meat is usually served as a main course after the obligatory *primo* of pasta, risotto, or soup. Popular everyday meat dishes, such as *scaloppine* of veal or pork, are quickly pan-fried in butter and served with a squeeze of lemon. In fact, it is not uncommon to have lemon wedges served alongside most fried or grilled meats in Italy.

Cotoletta impanatta is another popular quick meal, comprising thin slices of either veal, pork, chicken, or turkey, coated in breadcrumbs and shallow-fried. It is often enjoyed by children, but adults love it too! *La bistecca* (steak) is an all-time favorite and cooking slices of meat *alle brace* (on the barbecue) is popular during summer or when you have a crowd.

SALTIMBOCCA DI POLLO
CHICKEN SALTIMBOCCA WITH FONTINA, PROSCIUTTO, AND SAGE

Named for its irresistible taste—*saltimbocca* literally translates as "jump in the mouth"—this classic Roman speciality has become a popular meat dish all over the world. Originally made with veal, it can also be made with pork or chicken. Don't season the chicken, since you get saltiness from the prosciutto and tasty deliciousness from the sage and oozing Fontina. Serve with boiled potatoes and steamed greens for a delicious lunch or dinner.

Cooking time: 15 minutes (if chicken is already sliced)

Serves 4

12 oz/350 g chicken breast, thinly sliced into
   8 slices (you can ask your butcher
   to do this for you)
8 large sage leaves
1¾ oz/50 g Fontina, cut into 8 thin slices
8 slices of prosciutto, about 4½ oz/125 g total
3½ tbsp/1¾ oz/50 g butter
3 tbsp white wine

Place the chicken slices on a board (the slices should be no more than ¼-in/5-mm thick—if necessary, flatten with a meat mallet). Place a sage leaf in the middle of each one, followed by a slice of Fontina, and top with a slice of prosciutto, making sure the prosciutto covers the cheese. If your chicken slices are small, fold the prosciutto so that you have a double layer. Secure the ingredients in place with toothpicks inserted at an angle to ensure nothing falls off.

Melt 2 tablespoons/1 oz/30 g of the butter in a large frying pan set over medium heat. Add the *saltimbocca*, chicken-side down, and cook for 2 minutes, or until seared. Turn them over and cook for a further 2 minutes. Turn them over again, increase the heat to high, add the white wine, and cook for 1 minute. Remove the chicken and place on a serving dish. Add the remaining butter to the frying pan and cook for about 30 seconds, until creamy. Remove the toothpicks, pour the buttery sauce over the chicken, and serve immediately.

COSTOLLETTE DI AGNELLO ALL'ACCIUGA

ANCHOVY-INFUSED LAMB CHOPS

Lamb and anchovy is a match made in heaven, especially in this quick and simple dish using lamb rib chops. You can use chops that are on or off the bone, so the weight may vary. This dish makes a great mid-week supper, but is also perfect for a more formal meal when you have guests. It is delicious served with couscous or with some good bread to mop up the juices.

Cooking time: 25 minutes

Serves 4

8 lamb rib chops (about 1 lb/12 oz/800 g total)
3 tbsp extra-virgin olive oil
⅓ cup/80 ml white wine
2 garlic cloves, finely sliced
2 rosemary sprigs, needles only
leaves of 2 thyme sprigs
7 anchovy fillets
2 tbsp white wine vinegar

Place the lamb in a dish, drizzle with 1 tablespoon of olive oil, pour over the wine and scatter with the garlic and herbs. Set aside for 15 minutes for the flavors to infuse.

In a large frying pan set over medium heat, heat the remaining olive oil, add the anchovy fillets, and gently cook until the anchovy fillets dissolve. Increase the heat, add the lamb, and cook to sear well on both sides. Add the lamb marinade, cover with a lid, reduce the heat to medium, and cook for about 5 minutes, turning the lamb chops over from time to time.

Remove the lamb and place on a serving dish. Stir the vinegar into the sauce in the pan over medium heat, pour over the lamb, and serve.

COTOLETTE DI MAIALE RIPIENE DI SOTT'OLI

PORK STEAKS IN BREADCRUMBS WITH A PRESERVED VEGETABLE FILLING

Meat coated in breadcrumbs is always a popular meal in my house, especially among the children. To give the pork steaks a bit of a kick, my sister Adriana came up with the idea of filling them with some of my home-preserved vegetables. To prevent the filling from escaping, the meat has been double-dipped in egg and double-coated in breadcrumbs—this also gives it a crispier texture, which makes it all the more tasty. This is delicious served with Oregano-Infused Mixed Tomato Salad (see p.28) and lemon wedges, if desired, and can also be enjoyed cold, in-between some bread for a yummy sandwich.

Cooking time: 25 minutes (including prep)

Serves 4

4 pork steaks (about 1 lb 2 oz/500 g in total)
¾ cup/6¼ oz/180 g drained marinated
    artichokes, very finely chopped
6 sun-dried tomatoes preserved in oil,
    very finely chopped
8 black olives, very finely chopped
4 eggs
1½ tbsp grated Parmesan
sea salt and freshly ground black pepper
3 cups/11¼ oz/320 g breadcrumbs
4 tbsp/2 oz/60 g butter
½ cup/120 ml sunflower oil
lemon wedges, to serve (optional)

Slice the pork steaks horizontally in half, so you have 8 thin slices, lay them out flat on a board, and flatten each one out with a meat mallet as thinly as you can. Alternatively, you could ask your butcher to do this, to save time.

Top 4 of the slices of pork with the chopped artichokes, sun-dried tomatoes, and olives, then sandwich together with the other slices of pork, pressing down well.

Beat the eggs lightly in a bowl and combine with the grated Parmesan, seasoning with some salt and pepper. Place the breadcrumbs on a shallow plate. Carefully dip the filled pork steaks first in the egg mixture, then coat in the breadcrumbs. Repeat this one more time, so that all the steaks have a double coating.

Heat the butter and oil in a large frying pan set over medium–high heat and fry the filled pork steaks for about 5 minutes on each side. Remove and place on paper towels to drain any excess oil. Serve with lemon wedges and a tomato salad.

FEGATO CON CIPOLLE E UVETTA CON POLENTA SVELTA

CALVES' LIVER WITH ONIONS AND GOLDEN RAISINS, SERVED WITH QUICK POLENTA

I love calves' liver! It is so good for you, without the fat that most other cuts of meat contain. It is also extremely quick to cook and makes a tasty nutritious meal. This is my version of the classic *Fegato alla Veneziana,* where onions are steam-fried over gentle heat until transparent and softened. The addition of golden raisins here adds a pleasant sweetness. If you can't find calves' liver, substitute with pigs' or lambs' liver. This is delicious served with polenta, or mashed potatoes, if you prefer.

Cooking time: 25 minutes (not including prep)

Serves 4

1 tbsp golden raisins
scant ½ cup/100 ml white wine
¼ cup/60 ml extra-virgin olive oil
2 tbsp/1 oz/30 g butter
2 large onions, finely sliced
sea salt and freshly ground black pepper
1 lb/450 g calves' liver, cut into finger slices
a handful of parsley, finely chopped

For the polenta:
3½ cups/800 ml water
1⅓ cups/7 oz/200 g quick-cooking
    polenta cornmeal
a pat of butter
sea salt

Soak the golden raisins in the wine and set aside.

Heat the olive oil and butter in a frying pan set over low–medium heat. Add the onions and sweat for about 2 minutes. Add 2 tablespoons of water, season with some salt and pepper, cover with a lid, and cook over low heat for 10 minutes, until the onions have softened but not browned. Remove the onions and set aside.

Increase the heat to medium–high, add the pieces of liver, season with some salt and pepper, and sear well. Cover with a lid, reduce the heat to low–medium, and cook for about 7 minutes.

Meanwhile, make the polenta. Heat the water in a saucepan and cook the polenta (checking the instructions on your package), adding the butter and a little salt at the end.

Increase the heat under the frying pan with the liver, add the soaked raisins and white wine, and cook off the alcohol for a minute. Add the parsley and onions, heat through for a minute or so, then serve with the polenta.

INVOLTINI DI MAIALE
PORK INVOLTINI

These quick, rolled pork *involtini,* packed full of herbs and garlic, remind me of the delicious flavors of *porchetta.* Try to get the thinnest pork steaks you can, or ask your butcher to thinly cut and flatten them with a meat mallet, to save you time at home. They are delicious served with some boiled potatoes and a mixed green salad.

Cooking time: 30 minutes (including prep)

Serves 2–4

4 thinly cut pork escalopes or loin steaks
    (about 5 oz/140 g each)
sea salt and freshly ground black pepper
a handful of sage leaves, very finely chopped
1 rosemary sprig, needles only, very finely
    chopped
2 garlic cloves, very finely chopped
zest of ½ lemon
1½ tbsp grated Parmesan
2 tbsp extra-virgin olive oil
¼ cup/60 ml white wine

Lay the pork pieces out on a board, remove any excess fat, and flatten as thinly as you can with a meat mallet. Season with salt and pepper, and scatter the meat with the chopped herbs and garlic, followed by the lemon zest and grated Parmesan. Carefully roll up the pork slices to make 4 *involtini* and secure with toothpicks inserted at an angle.

In a large frying pan set over high heat, heat the olive oil, add the pork *involtini,* and cook to sear well on all sides. Add the white wine, cover with a lid, reduce the heat, and cook for 15 minutes. Remove from the heat, remove the toothpicks, and serve the *involtini* with the pan juices.

SCALOPPINE DI VITELLO CON PORRI E ARANCIE SANGUINELLO

PAN-FRIED VEAL WITH LEEKS AND BLOOD ORANGES

Veal *scaloppine* are very popular in Italy for a quick and easy meal, traditionally pan-fried with butter, sage, and lemon. As an alternative, I have used fresh thyme and delicious Sicilian blood oranges, which gives the meat a lovely, tangy kick! Unfortunately, these blood-red oranges are typically only available during the months of January and February, so, if making out of season, just substitute with regular oranges. The addition of leeks here means you don't have to prepare a side vegetable. Serve with lots of good crusty bread to mop up the delicious sauce.

Cooking time: 20 minutes

Serves 4

5 small blood oranges (zest of 2 oranges, juice
    of 1 orange; break the remaining 4 oranges
    into segments)
2 tbsp all-purpose flour
sea salt and freshly ground black pepper
4 veal escalopes (about 3½ oz/100 g each)
8 tbsp/4 oz/115 g butter
2 leeks, trimmed and finely sliced
4 fresh thyme sprigs
scant ½ cup/100 ml white wine

In a bowl, combine the orange zest with the flour, season with some salt and pepper, and set aside.

Lay the veal escalopes out flat on a board and flatten out further with a meat mallet, if necessary, and coat with the flour mixture, shaking off the excess. Set aside.

Melt half of the butter in a large frying pan set over medium heat. Add the leeks and sweat for 1 minute. Remove and set aside.

In the same pan, melt the remaining butter over medium heat, add the thyme, and leave to infuse for 1 minute. Increase the heat, add the veal, and sear well on both sides. Keep moving the meat around the pan to avoid burning. Pour in the wine and allow to evaporate by about half. Return the leeks to the pan, add the orange juice and half of the orange segments, and cook for 1 minute or so until the sauce begins to thicken slightly. Remove the meat, place on a serving dish, and pour the sauce over it. Serve immediately, garnished with the remaining fresh orange segments.

INVOLTINI DI BRESAOLA CON CAPRINO

BRESAOLA PARCELS FILLED WITH GOAT CHEESE AND CHIVES

Bresaola is a lovely cured beef that comes from the Valtellina area of northern Italy. Delicate in taste and extremely healthy, it is usually served as an antipasto with arugula, Parmesan, a drizzle of extra-virgin olive oil, and lemon juice. Here, to enrich the cured beef, a delicious mixture of goat cheese and chives is added. This can be served as a quick antipasto or as a light main course.

Cooking time: 10 minutes

Serves 4

4¼ oz/120 g soft goat cheese (chèvre)
1 tbsp extra-virgin olive oil, plus extra
    for drizzling
a handful of chives, finely chopped
sea salt and freshly ground black pepper
8 small slices of *bresaola* (about 1¾ oz/50 g
    in total)
juice of 1 lemon
8 whole chives, soaked
arugula leaves, to serve

In a bowl, combine the cheese, olive oil, and chopped chives, and season with some salt and pepper. Mix until creamy.

Place the slices of *bresaola* on a board or work surface and squeeze a little lemon juice over them. Place a small dollop of the creamy cheese mixture on each slice and wrap like a little parcel. Tie a soaked chive around each parcel to hold everything in place. Serve with arugula leaves, a drizzle of extra-virgin olive oil, and another drizzle of lemon juice.

FILETTI DI POLLO IN PADELLA
PAN-FRIED CHICKEN TENDERS

Chicken tenders, widely available in supermarkets, are very versatile and quick to cook. They can be added to stir-fries, made into quick stews, or dipped in egg and coated with breadcrumbs for the best home-made chicken nuggets. This is a quick, lighter version of a classic Chicken *Cacciatora*. Serve with some good rustic bread or boiled baby potatoes. For extra speed, look out for pre-chopped fresh vegetables.

Cooking time: 25 minutes (including prep)

Serves 4

3 tbsp extra-virgin olive oil
1 onion, finely sliced
½ fresh red chili pepper, finely chopped
2 celery stalks, finely chopped
1 large carrot, finely chopped
2 rosemary sprigs
1 lb 2 oz/500 g chicken tenders
sea salt and freshly ground black pepper
⅓ cup/80 ml white wine
1⅓ cups/7 oz/200 g baby plum tomatoes
a handful of basil leaves

Heat the olive oil in a frying pan set over medium heat. Add the onion, chili pepper, celery, carrot, and rosemary, and sweat for 2–3 minutes. Add the chicken tenders, season with some salt and pepper, and fry, stirring, until seared on all sides. Add the white wine and allow the alcohol to evaporate. Add the tomatoes and basil, reduce the heat, cover with a lid, and cook for 12–15 minutes, until the chicken has cooked through.

POLPETTONE FARCITO
ADRIANA'S FILLED MEATLOAF

This dish reminds me of home, where we would often have meatballs. However, meatballs take a little time to make, patiently rolling each one individually. When my mother was in a hurry, she would make a meatloaf with ground meat instead. This is my sister Adriana's version, filled with delicious mortadella, mozzarella, and hard-boiled eggs. Simple to prepare, it makes a nutritious meal, served with boiled baby potatoes and a green salad.

Cooking time: 40 minutes

Serves 4

3 eggs
9 oz/250 g good-quality ground beef
2 oz/60 g stale bread, soaked in a little milk
1½ tbsp grated Parmesan
1 tbsp parsley, finely chopped
1 rosemary sprig, needles only, finely chopped
sea salt and freshly ground black pepper
2 slices of mortadella (about 1 oz/30 g in total)
2½ oz/70 g firm mozzarella, thinly sliced
egg wash, made with 1 egg yolk and
    1 tbsp milk
breadcrumbs, for coating

ready-made loaf pan liner

Preheat the oven to 475°F/240°C, or your highest setting.

Boil 2 of the eggs until hard-boiled (about 7–8 minutes). When cooked, drain, remove the shells, and slice in half lengthways.

In the meantime, combine the ground beef, bread, Parmesan, parsley, rosemary, and 1 egg, and season with some salt and pepper. Place a piece of plastic wrap on your work surface and spread the beef mixture on top into a flat rectangular shape, about the length of your loaf pan liner. Lay over the mortadella slices, then the mozzarella slices, and top with the hard-boiled eggs. With the help of the plastic, roll it up into a sausage shape, then carefully remove and discard the plastic.

Brush egg wash all over the meatloaf and coat with the breadcrumbs. Place in a ready-made loaf pan liner (this helps the meatloaf keep its shape) and place onto a baking tray. Roast in the hot oven for 25 minutes, reducing the oven temperature to 425°F/220°C after 10 minutes.

Remove from the oven and serve with boiled baby potatoes and a mixed green salad.

BISTECCHE IN SALSA

STEAKS IN A HERB-INFUSED TOMATO SAUCE

When I was a child, this dish was often made as a quick supper during the late summer months, when tomatoes were ripe, ready, and at their best. Nowadays, people cook this classic southern-Italian dish with canned tomatoes all year round. If you cook some pasta separately to serve, it makes a really quick two-course meal for the whole family to enjoy.

Cooking time: 25–30 minutes

Serves 4

3 tbsp extra-virgin olive oil
4 thin beef steaks
1 large garlic clove, finely chopped
1 tsp capers
⅔ cup/2 oz/60 g pitted green olives
1 × 14-oz/400-g can of chopped tomatoes
a handful of basil leaves, plus a few extra to
    garnish (optional)
2 thyme sprigs
1 tsp dried oregano
sea salt and freshly ground black pepper
14 oz/400 g pasta of your choice

Heat the olive oil in a large frying pan set over medium heat. Add the steaks and cook to sear well on both sides, then remove and set aside.

In the same pan, add the garlic and sweat for about 30 seconds, stir in the capers and olives, and continue to sweat for another 30 seconds. Add the tomatoes, basil, thyme, and oregano, season with salt and pepper, and cook for a further 2 minutes. Return the steaks to the pan, cover with a lid, and continue to cook over medium heat for 20 minutes.

While the meat is cooking in the tomato sauce, bring a saucepan of salted water to a boil and cook some pasta. Serve the cooked pasta stirred though the tomato and olive sauce, with the meat as a main course. Garnish with a few extra chopped basil leaves, if you wish.

VEGETABLES

Italy is blessed with a wonderful variety of vegetables, and each region has its own locally-grown varieties, which, in season, are excellent for the traditional dishes of that particular area. The Mediterranean climate and the difference between the cooler north and warmer south makes it ideal for growing all kinds of different produce—the north has its root vegetables and the south its tomatoes, bell peppers, eggplants, and more.

Italians don't just eat veggies as a side dish, although there is always seasonal vegetables or salad served at the table—we make wonderful main course dishes out of them too. Born from the *cucina povera*, in the days when poor people had to make do with the few ingredients they had available to them, wonderful dishes were created. Vegetables were often filled with leftovers and stale bread and made into substantial main courses—these dishes are still popular today and have become real delicacies.

Vegetables are quick to cook, very versatile, and can be made into delicious side dishes and main meals in no time. They provide lots of vital nutrients and vitamins and, quite frankly, I don't know how I could live without them.

Even though I prefer to eat seasonally—not only are veggies more economical that way, but they taste better too—we are lucky to find all kinds of produce available at almost any time of the year, which makes cooking dishes much easier. And when you're really under pressure time-wise, you can buy pre-prepared veg, such as trimmed green beans or chopped peppers, which can just go straight into the pan and save much preparation time.

FRITTATA CON PISELLI, PECORINO E MENTA

FRITTATA WITH PEAS, PECORINO, AND FRESH MINT

Italians often have frittata for an evening meal (usually as a main course after a plate of pasta or soup). Frittata is nutritious, quick, and easy to make, and can be enjoyed cold the next day as a *panino*—in between some bread. Serve with Oregano-Infused Mixed Tomato Salad (see p.28) for a healthy supper.

Cooking time: 15 minutes

Serves 4

3 tbsp extra-virgin olive oil
2 large *cipollotti* (spring onions), or 4 large
    scallions, finely chopped
12 mint leaves
2 cups/10½ oz/300 g frozen peas
1 tbsp water
8 eggs
2 tbsp milk
1 tbsp breadcrumbs
generous ½ cup/1½ oz/40 g grated Pecorino
sea salt and freshly ground black pepper,
    to taste

Heat the olive oil in a large, non-stick frying pan set over medium heat. Add the onions and a couple of mint leaves and sweat for 2 minutes. Stir in the peas and water and cook for 2–3 minutes, until the liquid has evaporated and the peas are tender.

Meanwhile, mix the eggs, milk, breadcrumbs, Pecorino, the remaining mint leaves, and some salt and pepper. Pour the eggy mixture over the peas and cook as you would an omelet, turning halfway through, until set firm and golden. If you find you can't turn the frittata over, place under a hot broiler for a few minutes, until golden and cooked.

VERDURE MISTE STUFATE

MIXED VEGGIE STEW

This quick, delicious vegetable stew can be served as an accompaniment to meat dishes or can be eaten as a main course with some steamed rice or bread. If you are in a hurry, most of these vegetables can be found pre-chopped in lots of supermarkets.

Cooking time: 25 minutes (not including vegetable prep)

Serves 4

3 tbsp extra-virgin olive oil
1 small red onion, finely sliced
1 small carrot, finely chopped
½ red bell pepper, finely chopped into thin strips
½ yellow bell pepper, finely chopped into thin strips
½ green bell pepper, finely chopped into thin strips
7 oz/200 g ripe tomatoes, coarsely chopped
3½ oz/100 g fine green beans, trimmed
7 oz/200 g zucchini, finely sliced
7 oz/200 g eggplant, finely chopped into small cubes
1 potato, peeled and cut into small chunks
2 rosemary sprigs
2 thyme sprigs
1 tsp black peppercorns
scant 1 cup/200 ml vegetable stock
½ handful of parsley, coarsely chopped

Heat the olive oil in an extra-large saucepan set over medium heat. Add the onion and sweat for 2 minutes. Stir in all of the other vegetables, and the rosemary, thyme, and peppercorns. Cook for 1 minute or so, to allow the flavors to infuse. Pour in the stock, cover with a lid, and cook for 20 minutes.

Check the stew about 5 minutes before the end of the cooking time. If you find there is still too much liquid, increase the heat and cook uncovered, so that the liquid can reduce slightly. Remove from the heat, stir in the chopped parsley, and serve.

ZUCCHINI IN POMODORO

ZUCCHINI IN TOMATO

Zucchini can be quite bland, so cooking them in a little tomato sauce gives them the kick they need to make a tasty side dish. It can be served with meat dishes or by itself with some crusty bread.

Cooking time: 25 minutes

Serves 4

2 tbsp extra-virgin olive oil
1 onion, finely chopped
⅓ cup/1¾ oz/50 g diced pancetta
1 lb 2 oz/500 g zucchini, cut into small chunks
6 basil leaves
¾ cup/7 oz/200 g canned chopped tomatoes
sea salt and freshly ground black pepper

Heat the olive oil in a large saucepan set over medium heat. Add the onion and pancetta and fry, stirring, for about 4 minutes, until the onion has softened and the pancetta has colored a little. Stir in the zucchini and basil and fry, stirring, for 1 minute. Add the tomatoes, season with some salt and pepper, cover with a lid, and cook over low heat for about 10–15 minutes, stirring from time to time, until the zucchini are tender.

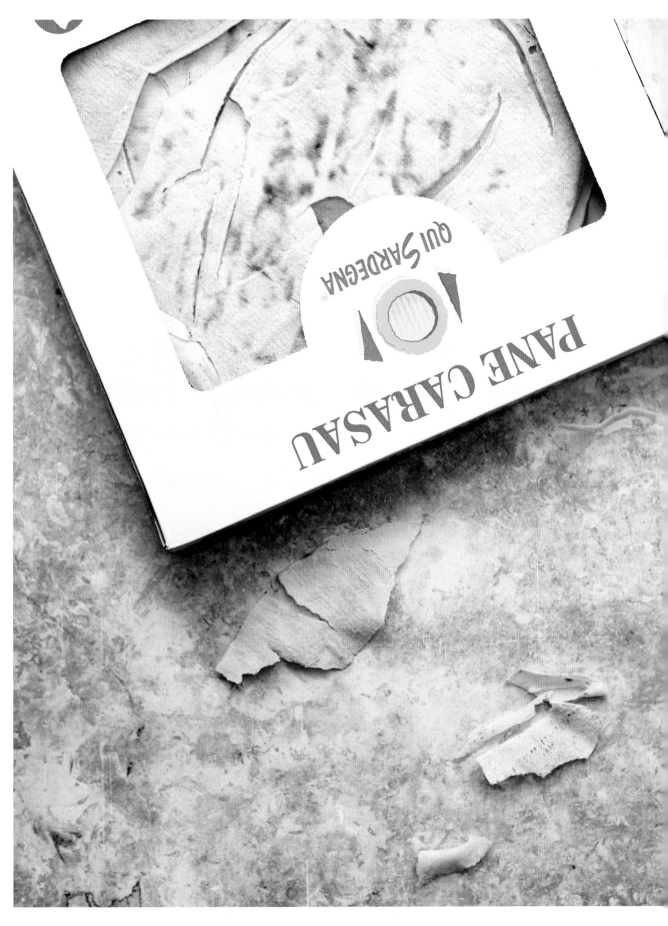

PIZZA VELOCE AL PANE CARASAU

QUICK PIZZA WITH SARDINIAN CRISPY BREAD

Pane carasau, also known as *carta di musica*, is a crispy, unleavened flatbread, which was made for Sardinian shepherds to take with them to the mountains to eat during their working day. Its crispness makes it a light alternative to bread, and its long shelf life makes it an ideal pantry ingredient. You can find it in your local Italian deli.

This quick, pizza-type recipe makes a great snack when time is precious or for when impromptu guests appear. The addition of potatoes makes it quite filling, but you could use any of your favorite pizza toppings. When serving, I find a sharp pair of kitchen scissors the best tool to cut it with, since the bread is quite crispy.

Cooking time: 20–25 minutes (including prep)

Makes 2 large pizzas

1 lb 5 oz/600 g potatoes, peeled and
    thinly sliced
sea salt
1 red onion, finely sliced
a pinch of oregano
⅔ cup/3½ oz/100 g cherry tomatoes, quartered
extra-virgin olive oil, for drizzling
2 large *pane carasau* (from your local
    Italian deli)
3½ oz/100 g mozzarella, coarsely chopped

Preheat the oven to 400°F/200°C.

Place the sliced potatoes in a saucepan of salted boiling water and cook for 5–6 minutes, until tender, but not falling apart. Drain well, taking care not to break them.

Meanwhile, prepare the other ingredients. Combine the sliced onion in a bowl with a little seasoning of salt and oregano. Mix the tomatoes in a separate bowl with a little salt and a drizzle of extra-virgin olive oil.

Place each *pane carasau* on a large baking sheet and drizzle each with a little extra-virgin olive oil. Place the sliced potatoes on top, followed by some onions, mozzarella, and tomatoes, finishing off with another drizzle of olive oil. Place in the hot oven for 6–8 minutes, until the mozzarella has melted, and serve immediately.

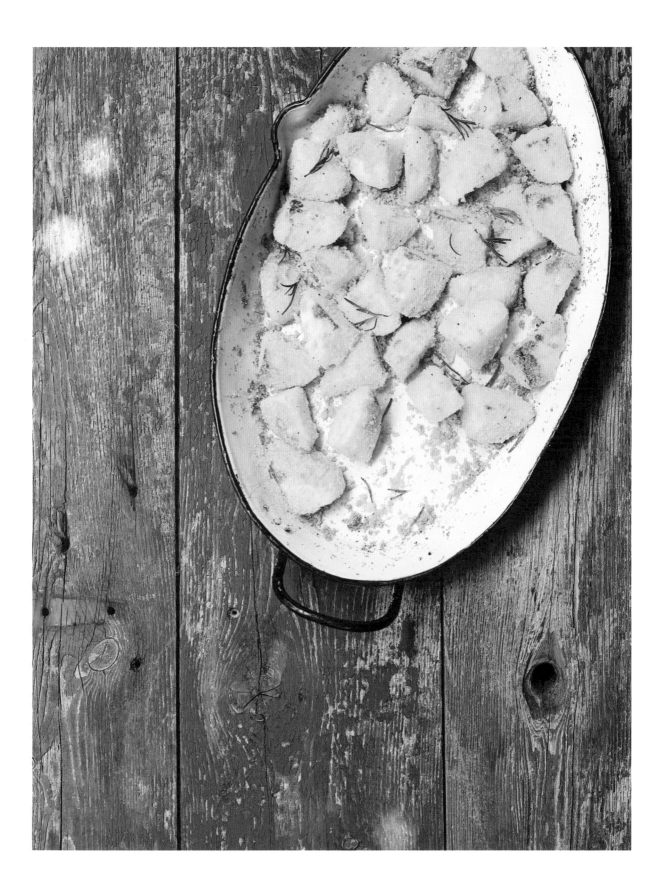

PATATE AL PARMIGIANO E ROSMARINO

PARMESAN ROAST POTATOES WITH ROSEMARY

This is an alternative but wonderful way to serve roast potatoes. The Parmesan and cornmeal mixture adds a nice crunchiness, and the roasted rosemary is delicious to eat, as well as giving the dish a fantastic flavor. To cook this even more quickly, chop the potatoes into smaller chunks. It makes a lovely accompaniment to steaks and meat cutlets.

Cooking time: 30–35 minutes

Serves 4–6

2 lb 4 oz/1 kg potatoes, peeled and cut into
    small chunks
¾ cup/1¾ oz/50 g grated Parmesan
¾ cup/3½ oz/100 g fine cornmeal
sea salt and freshly ground black pepper
2 tbsp extra-virgin olive oil,
    plus extra for drizzling
2 rosemary sprigs, needles only

Preheat the oven to 425°F/220°C.

Place the potatoes in a large saucepan of water, bring to a boil, and parboil for 5–6 minutes.

Meanwhile, in a bowl, combine the Parmesan, cornmeal, and some salt and pepper and set aside.

Drain the potatoes well and let them steam-dry for a minute or so over low heat to eliminate the excess moisture.

Add the olive oil to an oven dish, add the potatoes, and mix well to coat the potatoes in oil. Add the Parmesan mixture and mix again, until the potatoes are well coated. Scatter in the rosemary and drizzle with some more olive oil.

Place in the hot oven and roast for about 25 minutes, until cooked through and golden.

CAVOLFIORE AL FORNO

ROASTED CAULIFLOWER WITH LEMON, PAPRIKA, AND BAY LEAVES

I love cauliflower and enjoy cooking it in many different ways. Roasting this root vegetable is now becoming popular in Italy, and exotic spices are often used as flavoring. This is my own version, using Italian ingredients and some paprika. For an added kick, you could substitute the paprika with red pepper flakes. Quick and simple to prepare, it makes a lovely side to meat dishes, or, if you're like me, it's delicious to eat on its own!

Cooking time: 30 minutes (including prep)

Serves 4–6

1 lb 2 oz/500 g cauliflower florets
2 bay leaves, finely chopped
3 garlic cloves, left whole and squashed
2 tsp smoked paprika
sea salt
juice of 1 lemon
¼ cup/60 ml extra-virgin olive oil

Preheat the oven to 400°F/200°C.

Combine all the ingredients in a baking dish and roast in the hot oven for 25 minutes, until cooked through.

AGRODOLCE DI VERDURE AL ZAFFERANO

SAFFRON-INFUSED AGRODOLCE VEGETABLE STIR-FRY

The slightly sweet and sour flavor of the vinegar and sugar here gives a nice kick to the vegetables, and the saffron adds a hint of color. This makes a lovely accompaniment to grilled meat, but is also delicious eaten on its own.

Cooking time: 25 minutes (including prep)

Serves 4

⅓ cup/80 ml extra-virgin olive oil
2 garlic cloves, left whole and squashed
1 large red onion, finely sliced
4¼ oz/120 g celery heart, sliced
10½ oz/300 g rainbow chard, sliced
9 oz/250 g turnips, peeled and diced
6 oz/170 g baby broccoli, trimmed
3 tbsp white wine vinegar
2 tsp sugar
a pinch of saffron strands

Heat 2 tablespoons of the olive oil in a small frying pan set over low heat. Add the garlic and onions and gently sweat for about 7 minutes.

At the same time, in a larger frying pan set over medium–high heat, heat the rest of the olive oil, add the celery, rainbow chard, turnips, and broccoli and stir-fry for about 10 minutes.

Combine the white wine vinegar, sugar, and saffron, pour this over the vegetables, and allow the alcohol to cook off. Stir in the onion (discard the garlic), and heat through for a final minute, before serving.

CAPPUCCIA POVERA AL FORNO

POOR MAN'S CABBAGE BAKE

This recipe is so typical of the days of *cucina povera*, when poor people made do with whatever ingredients were available to them, and bread was often used to make a meal go further. Simple, but nutritious, this can be served as a side dish to meat, but it is just as delicious eaten as a main course.

Cooking time: 40 minutes (including prep)

Serves 2–4

1 pointed (sweetheart) cabbage, or ½ green
   cabbage (14 oz/400 g total), coarsely
   chopped into thick strips
sea salt
3½ oz/100 g rustic bread,
   such as sourdough
4½ oz/125 g mozzarella
3 tbsp extra-virgin olive oil,
   plus extra for drizzling
1 garlic clove, left whole
a few pinches of paprika

Preheat the oven to 400°F/200°C.

Cook the cabbage in salted boiling water for about 7 minutes, then drain (keeping a ladle or so of the cooking water).

Meanwhile, chop the bread into cubes, and roughly slice the mozzarella, and set aside.

Heat the olive oil in a frying pan set over medium heat. Add the garlic and sweat for a minute or so. Add the drained cabbage to the pan, seasoning with a little salt and a pinch of paprika, and fry, stirring, for 4 minutes.

Place the cooked cabbage, bread cubes, and mozzarella in a baking dish, add a ladle of cooking water, a drizzle of olive oil, and a sprinkle of paprika, and bake in the hot oven for 20 minutes.

Meanwhile preheat the broiler.

Remove the dish from the oven and place under the hot broiler for 4 minutes, until golden-brown. Serve immediately.

TORTINO DI BIETOLE CON UOVA
BREAKFAST, LUNCH, AND DINNER!

A delicious bake of chard, eggs, and cheese, the English title of this recipe sums up the fact that you can enjoy this dish at any time of day! Very quick and simple to prepare, it makes a nutritious breakfast as well as a light supper. Be careful not to add salt to the creamy mixture, because the olive tapenade tends to be quite salty already. If you prefer, you could omit the tapenade and serve the toasted bread with a little salt and a drizzle of extra-virgin olive oil instead.

Cooking time: 20 minutes (including prep)

Serves 4

14 oz/400 g rainbow chard, washed
   and trimmed
sea salt, for the cooking water
butter, for greasing
small jar of black olive tapenade
4 eggs, carefully separated (try to keep the
   yolks whole)
scant ½ cup/100 ml heavy cream
freshly ground black pepper
generous ½ cup/1½ oz/40 g grated Parmesan
slices of sourdough bread, to serve

4 × 6-in/15-cm round terracotta dishes

Preheat the oven to 350°F/180°C.

Add the chard to a saucepan of salted boiling water and cook for 5 minutes.

Meanwhile, grease 4 × 6-in/15-cm round terracotta dishes with butter and spread a little of the black olive tapenade, to taste, in the bottom of each.

Whisk together the egg whites, cream, black pepper, and grated Parmesan, until well combined and creamy.

Drain the chard and divide among the terracotta dishes, overlapping the leaves if necessary to fit into the dishes. Pour on the creamy mixture and bake in the hot oven for 7 minutes. After this time, remove from the oven and carefully add an egg yolk on top of each dish. Return to the oven for 2–3 minutes, until the egg is cooked but still soft.

Lightly toast the bread slices, spread with a little of the olive paste, and serve with the egg and chard bakes.

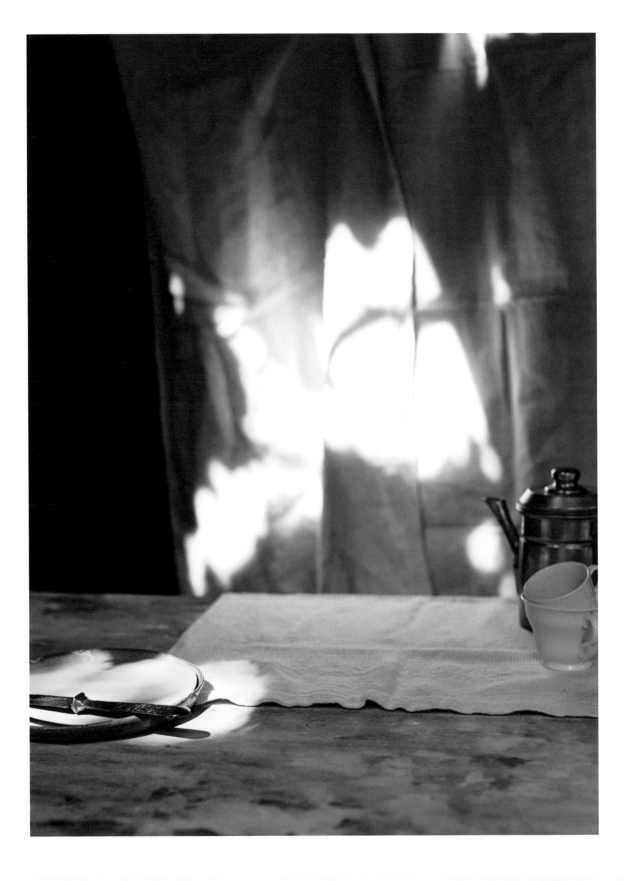

LATTUGA RIPIENA

FILLED LETTUCE

In Southern Italy, where *escarole*—a type of lettuce—is widely grown, it is quite common to serve it like this. The idea originated in the days of *cucina povera* (peasant cooking), when local vegetables would be filled with whatever ingredients were available, to make the meal go further. These crunchy lettuces can be served as an appetizer, side, or main.

Cooking time: 20 minutes

Serves 2–4

1 tbsp extra-virgin olive oil,
   plus extra for drizzling
1 garlic clove, left whole
½ fresh red chili pepper, finely chopped
1¾ cups/3½ oz/100 g breadcrumbs
¼ cup/1 oz/30 g pine nuts
½ cup/2 oz/60 g green and black pitted olives,
   halved or quartered, depending on size
salt and freshly ground black pepper
2 romaine lettuces

Preheat the oven to 400°F/200°C.

Heat a frying pan over low-medium heat, add the olive oil, and sauté the garlic and chili pepper for 1 minute, being careful not to let them burn. Add the breadcrumbs and pine nuts and cook for 3 minutes, until lightly toasted. Remove from the heat, discard the garlic clove, then stir in the olives. Season with a little salt and pepper.

Slightly open each lettuce and fill with the breadcrumb mixture, tucking it down in the center and in between the leaves. Place each lettuce on a sheet of parchment paper, drizzle all over with some olive oil, then wrap the lettuce up tightly in the paper—like a huge hard candy! Place on a baking tray and bake in the hot oven for 8 minutes.

Remove from the oven and carefully open the parcels. Slice the lettuces in half lengthways and serve.

FAGIOLINI IN UOVO AL SUCCO DI LIMONE

EGGY GREEN BEANS WITH LEMON

I remember seeing this dish made at a farmhouse in Puglia—the green beans were freshly picked from their garden and the eggs were fresh from their chickens. I remember thinking it was such a simple recipe, but the flavors were out of this world. I have tried to recreate it for this book. Although it is typically served as a side dish to meat, I could quite happily eat a bowlful with some country bread.

Cooking time: 20 minutes

Serves 4

1 lb 2 oz/500 g green beans, trimmed
1½ tbsp/¾ oz/20 g butter
1 tbsp extra-virgin olive oil
sea salt and freshly ground black pepper
1 egg, lightly beaten
juice of ½ lemon

Cook the beans in boiling water for 10–15 minutes, until tender, then drain.

In a large frying pan, heat the butter and olive oil over high heat, add the drained beans, season with salt and pepper, and fry, stirring, for 1 minute. Reduce the heat to medium, then add the beaten egg and lemon juice, stirring well. Remove from the heat and serve immediately.

SIMPLE SAUCES

Delicious Italian food can be prepared in an instant by adding tomato sauce or pesto to quickly prepared meat, fish, and vegetable dishes, pasta, soups, and salads. In this section are two of my favorite sauce recipes to make ahead and store, or, if you need to make a sauce in a hurry, to adorn whatever you are preparing.

SALSA AL POMODORO
BASIC TOMATO SAUCE

There are so many good-quality tomato sauces on the market now, especially the fresh ones sold in Italian delis, but I always like to make my own. This is my version of a plain, simple tomato sauce, which can be used to dress pasta or add to many other dishes. When you have time, it's always worth making a batch or two to freeze and use later. It will keep fresh in the refrigerator for up to 3 days.

Cooking time: 25 minutes (including prep)

Makes approx. 3 cups/1 lb 8 oz/680 g

2 tbsp extra-virgin olive oil
½ onion, finely chopped
2 × 14-oz/400-g cans of chopped plum
    tomatoes
sea salt
handful of basil, roughly torn

Heat the olive oil in a saucepan set over medium heat, add the onion, and sweat for a couple of minutes. Add the chopped tomatoes and some water (about half a tomato can), some salt to taste, and the basil. Cover the pan with a lid and simmer over low–medium heat for about 20 minutes. Check for seasoning and use accordingly.

PESTO

PESTO SAUCE

Pesto is always handy to keep in the refrigerator so you can whip up a quick meal in no time. Add it to cooked pasta or gnocchi, liven up vegetable soups, add it to omelets, or simply use it in sandwiches. It will keep in the refrigerator for about a week or it can be frozen. If you store pesto in the refrigerator, make sure you add some extra-virgin olive oil to the top and cover with plastic wrap. I usually make pesto the old-fashioned way with a mortar and pestle, which doesn't take that long and means the pesto retains a slight crunchiness, but you can also make it in a food processor, which takes no time at all.

Cooking time: 15 minutes by hand/5 minutes in a food processor

Makes 4 servings, to dress pasta or gnocchi

2 tbsp pine nuts
1 garlic clove
½ tsp coarse sea salt
2¾ oz/80 g fresh basil leaves
   (discard the stalks)
scant 1 cup/200 ml good-quality
   extra-virgin olive oil
2 tbsp freshly grated Parmesan

Put the pine nuts, garlic, and sea salt into a mortar and grind with a pestle. Add a few basil leaves and some olive oil, grinding and stirring with the pestle. Continue this procedure until you have used up all the basil leaves and about half of the olive oil, and have obtained a smooth, silky consistency. Add the remaining olive oil and the Parmesan and combine well.

Alternatively, place all the ingredients in a food processor and blend.

DESSERTS

When planning meals, people often overlook desserts, thinking they take too long or are just too hard to tackle, instead opting for a store-bought dessert or cake. Desserts don't have to take a long time to prepare to be impressive or delicious—sometimes the quickest and simplest are the best.

I remember as a child, my favorite sweet treat was fresh ricotta, simply combined with a little sugar and cinnamon or perhaps some chocolate chips or dried fruit. Ricotta is used in a lot of Italian desserts, as a filling for tarts and pies, or in classic pastries such as Sicilian *cannoli* and *cassata*. More recently, mascarpone—the rich, creamy cheese used to make tiramisu—has taken over in popularity and this, too, is now added to many desserts.

Fruit has always been a popular dessert in Italy and most families will offer a bowl of seasonal fruit after a meal so everyone can help themselves. Fruit is good for you, packed with vitamins, provides a natural source of sugar, and is often included in many Italian tarts and cakes. The classic *macedonia di frutta* (fruit salad), drizzled with a little freshly squeezed lemon or orange juice, is always a welcome dessert in Italy—it takes little time to prepare and provides a healthy, light, and refreshing end to a meal.

I hope you will enjoy recreating my quick and simple dessert ideas, all of which can be made just before serving. Most can also be prepared in advance, if you prefer.

AMARETTI RIPIENI

FILLED SOFT AMARETTI

Soft amaretti, or *amaretti morbidi* in Italian, are like little cakes and are not to be confused with the hard, crispy variety of amaretti. Made with ground almonds, they are gluten-free (although always check the package) and are obtainable in Italian delis or in larger supermarkets. They are delicious eaten on their own; filled with a rich, creamy center, they also make a lovely, quick dessert. If you can't find raw pistachios, substitute with walnuts, chocolate chips, candied fruit, or a combination, if desired.

Cooking time: 20 minutes (including prep)

Makes 12–24 (depending on size!)

2½ tbsp raw pistachios
⅓ cup/2½ oz/75 g ricotta
⅓ cup/2½ oz/75 g mascarpone
heaped 1 tbsp sugar
3 tsp Marsala wine, plus extra for brushing
20–24 soft amaretti cookies
a little confectioners' sugar, for dusting

Toast the pistachios in a dry frying pan set over medium–high heat for a couple of minutes, until lightly toasted. Remove and set aside.

Meanwhile, whisk together the ricotta, mascarpone, sugar, and Marsala wine in a bowl, until light and fluffy. Finely chop the pistachios and stir them in. Cover with plastic wrap and place in the refrigerator.

Using a really good, sharp knife, slice the amaretti horizontally in half, so you end up with a bottom and top of each little cake, keeping any crumbs. Brush each slice with a little Marsala. Take the creamy mixture out of the refrigerator and stir in the amaretti crumbs. Place a dollop of the cream on the bottom slice of the amaretti and sandwich together with the top half. Arrange on a plate and dust with confectioners' sugar, to serve.

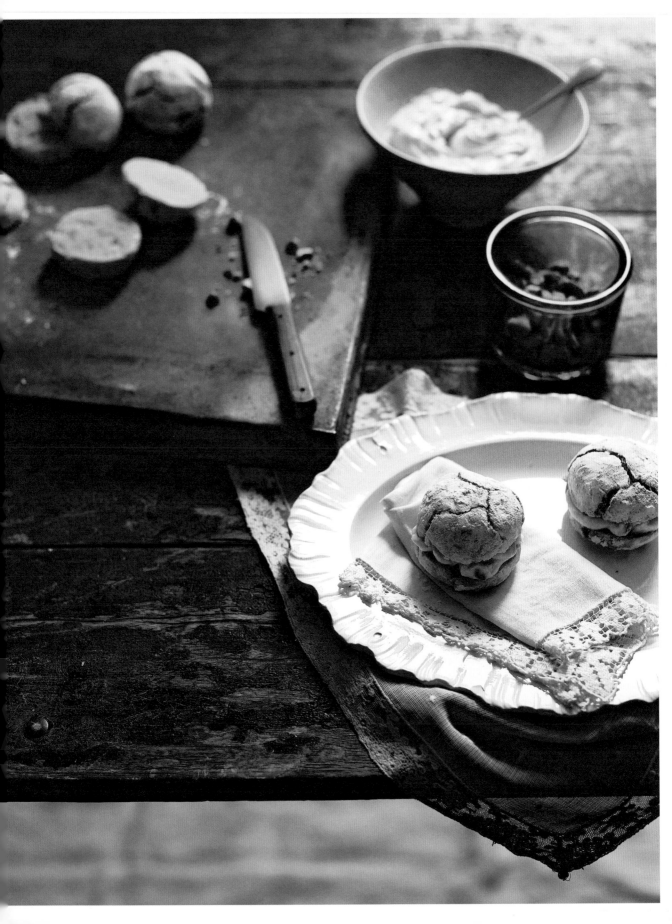

BUDINO AL CIOCCOLATO E LAMPONI

CHOCOLATE AND RASPBERRY POTS

These quick, soufflé-type chocolate puddings are so easy to make, they are almost child's play. But *shhh*, don't tell your guests—they'll think you've been slaving in the kitchen for hours when they taste them! You can make them in advance and put them in the microwave for about 20–30 seconds each, just before serving. Make sure you use good-quality, organic dark or bittersweet chocolate and fresh raspberries. Simply eat with a spoon, straight out of the ramekin or cup!

Cooking time: 25 minutes

Serves 4

4 tbsp/2 oz/60 g butter,
    plus extra for greasing
4½ oz/125 g dark or bittersweet chocolate,
    broken into pieces
3 eggs, separated (keep 2 egg yolks,
    1 can be saved for later use or discarded)
2 tbsp sugar
a pinch of table salt
scant 1 cup/3½ oz/100 g raspberries

Preheat the oven to 350°F/180°C. Lightly grease 4 ramekins or cappuccino cups, place them on a flat baking tray, and set aside.

Melt the chocolate pieces and butter in a heatproof bowl set over a pan of gently simmering water. Make sure the base of the bowl doesn't touch the water.

Meanwhile, in another bowl, whisk 2 egg yolks with 1 tablespoon of the sugar, until light and creamy.

In another very clean bowl, whisk the 3 egg whites with the remaining sugar and a pinch of salt, until stiff.

Combine the melted chocolate mixture with the egg yolk mixture. Now, fold in the stiffened egg whites, until well incorporated. Pour into the prepared ramekins/cups up to about halfway, gently place 3–4 raspberries in each, pushing them in a little, then pour the remaining chocolate mixture over to cover. Bake in the hot oven for 6 minutes. Remove and serve.

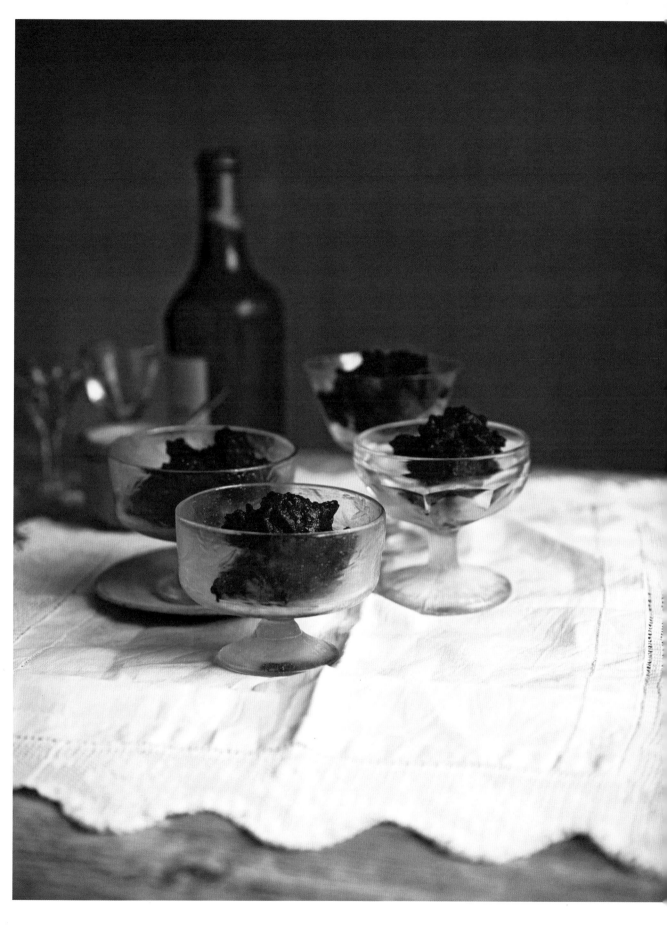

SORBETTO DI FRUTTI DI BOSCO VELOCE

QUICK MIXED BERRY SORBET

Quick and easy to make, this sorbet is made with frozen mixed berries, which are widely obtainable in supermarkets. Alternatively, you can freeze the berries that you pick or grow yourself during the summer—they are always handy to have in the freezer, so you can whip up a healthy dessert at any time. My daughter Olivia loves this idea and makes sorbets of all kinds with different types of frozen fruit. I have given you a few serving suggestions, but you can adapt to whatever you prefer or simply enjoy the sorbet by itself.

Cooking time: 5 minutes

Serves 4–6

2¾ cups/1 lb 2 oz/500 g frozen mixed berries
juice of 1 orange
½ cup/3½ oz/100 g sugar

Serving suggestions:
crushed amaretti cookies
Pavesini (Italian lady fingers)
fresh fruit, such as sliced kiwi or mango
crème fraîche or whipped cream

Place all the ingredients into a food processor and blend until smooth. Serve immediately, with the above serving suggestions or your own ideas.

CREMA DI MASCARPONE CON PERE E NOCI

MASCARPONE MOUSSE WITH PEAR AND WALNUTS

This is a very quick, simple, and delicious dessert! The cream is quite indulgent and combines really well with my favorite fruit and nuts: soft, sweet pears and crunchy walnuts. A perfect dinner party dessert, this looks lovely served in glasses or glass bowls.

Cooking time: 10 minutes

Serves 4–6

5 ripe Bosc pears, peeled and cored
⅓ cup/1½ oz/40 g walnut halves
generous 1 cup/9 oz/250 g mascarpone
generous 1 cup/9 oz/250 g cream cheese
scant ½ cup/100 ml heavy cream
2 tbsp superfine sugar
runny honey, for drizzling

Chop 4 of the pears into small chunks and divide among 4–6 bowls or glasses. Slice the remaining pears into 4–6 pieces and set aside.

Roughly break up the walnuts, keeping 4–6 intact for decoration. Place the broken walnut pieces in the bowls or glasses with the pears.

In a bowl, combine the mascarpone, cream cheese, cream, and sugar, and mix with a spoon until smooth. Spoon this creamy mixture over the chopped pears and walnuts in the bowls or glasses. Drizzle with a little honey and decorate with the remaining pieces of pear and walnuts. Serve immediately, or refrigerate until required.

MERINGA CON CREMA DI LIMONE E FRUTTI DI BOSCO

MERINGUE NESTS WITH LEMON CUSTARD AND BERRIES

Ready-made meringue cookies and nests can be found in specialty food stores and, since they usually have a long sell-by-date, are great to keep in your pantry to use for a speedy dessert. Meringue goes so well with this quick-to-prepare, lemon-infused custard. If you are in a hurry, you could omit the cooling time and just spoon the hot custard onto the nests. They are delicious and look really lovely.

Cooking time: 35–40 minutes (including cooling time)

Makes 6

1 cup/250 ml whole milk
2-in/5-cm piece of lemon peel
1 tbsp limoncello liqueur
3 egg yolks
¼ cup/1¾ oz/50 g sugar
¼ cup/1 oz/30 g all-purpose flour, sifted
selection of fresh berries: strawberries, raspberries, blueberries, blackberries
6 ready-made meringue nests or extra-large meringue cookies

Heat the milk, lemon peel, and limoncello in a small saucepan over low heat—be careful not to let it boil.

Meanwhile, in a large bowl, whisk together the eggs yolks and sugar until light and fluffy. Whisk in the sifted flour.

When the milk is hot, gradually pour it into the egg mixture, whisking all the time. Return the mixture to the pan over low–medium heat and cook, stirring well with a wooden spoon, until the custard thickens. Pour into a cold dish, remove the piece of lemon peel, and set aside to cool for about 15 minutes.

Slice the strawberries, if using, and arrange the meringue nests on a large serving plate or board. Once cool, place the custard cream into a pastry bag and pipe onto the meringue nests—or you can just spoon it on. Top with the mixed berries and serve.

PESCHE AL PASSITO CON MASCARPONE

PASSITO-INFUSED PEACHES WITH MASCARPONE

For this dish, use just-ripe, delicious, sweet peaches in season, when they are at their best. Delicious served warm, you can also prepare all the ingredients in advance and just heat the peaches through in the cooking liquid before serving. The warm peaches go really well with the mascarpone cream, or you could serve with good-quality vanilla ice cream, if desired. *Passito di Pantelleria* is an exquisite dessert wine from the Sicilian island of Pantelleria. If you can't find it, substitute with Vin Santo, Marsala, or another sweet dessert wine.

Cooking time: 20–25 minutes (including prep)

Serves 4–6

6 tbsp/90 ml *Passito di Pantelleria* or
    sweet dessert wine
2 tbsp freshly squeezed orange juice
3½ tbsp light brown or raw sugar
4 peaches
⅔ cup/5½ oz/150 g mascarpone
3 tbsp confectioners' sugar, sifted

Combine 5 tablespoons of the *Passito* with the orange juice and brown sugar, and set aside.

Place the peaches in boiling water for about 30 seconds. Remove with a slotted spoon and plunge straight into ice-cold water to cool them. Once cooled, use a paring knife to peel away the skin, then cut the peaches into segments, about 8 per peach. Place the peach segments into the *Passito* liquid and leave to macerate for 10 minutes.

Meanwhile, combine the mascarpone, confectioners' sugar, and remaining *Passito*, and set aside.

Place the macerated peaches and their liquid into a small saucepan, bring to a boil, and simmer over medium heat for 5 minutes. Carefully remove the peaches and divide among 4–6 dessert bowls or glasses. Return the liquid to the heat and cook over high heat for a couple of minutes, until it reduces and thickens.

Top the peaches with dollops of the mascarpone mixture, drizzle with the reduced liquid, and serve immediately.

GIRANDOLE ALLA CANNELLA

CINNAMON PUFFS

These are really easy and quick-to-make cookies, which can be made at any time, then stored in an airtight container. They are delicious served at teatime. Try to get ready-rolled puff pastry, which will save you time rolling out. The ground cinnamon can be substituted with pumpkin pie spice.

Cooking time: 30 minutes

Makes about 15

generous ½ cup/4¼ oz/120 g light brown
   or raw sugar
3 tsp ground cinnamon
9 oz/250 g pre-rolled sheet of puff pastry
1 egg white, lightly beaten

Preheat the oven to 375°F/190°C. Line a large, flat baking sheet with parchment paper.

Combine the sugar and cinnamon in a bowl.

Unroll the puff pastry sheet and sprinkle about three-quarters of the sugar mixture all over. Roll the pastry up along the longest side, brush all over with the beaten egg white, and sprinkle with the remaining sugar mixture. Cut the roll into approx. ¾-in/2-cm thick rounds, place them on the prepared baking tray, and bake in the hot oven for 20 minutes, until golden.

MACEDONIA DI AGRUMI CON YOGURT SPEZIATO

CITRUS FRUIT SALAD WITH A CINNAMON YOGURT

This makes a lovely, healthy dessert that is full of vitamin C! You can either serve the fruit in a large bowl with the yogurt on the side, for people to help themselves, or you can divide among individual bowls and dollop the yogurt on top. Add more cinnamon if you prefer.

Cooking time: 15 minutes (including prep time)

Serves 4–6

1 yellow grapefruit
1 pink grapefruit
2 oranges
juice and zest of 1 lime
a grating of fresh ginger
1 tbsp clear honey
scant 1 cup/7 oz/200 g plain yogurt
a pinch of ground cinnamon
mint leaves, to garnish

Peel the citrus fruit, removing as much of the white pith as possible, then split into segments and place in a bowl. Combine the lime juice, grated ginger, and honey and pour over the fruit. Set aside.

Combine the yogurt and cinnamon. Divide the fruit between 4–6 bowls, top with the yogurt, and garnish with lime zest and mint leaves, to serve.

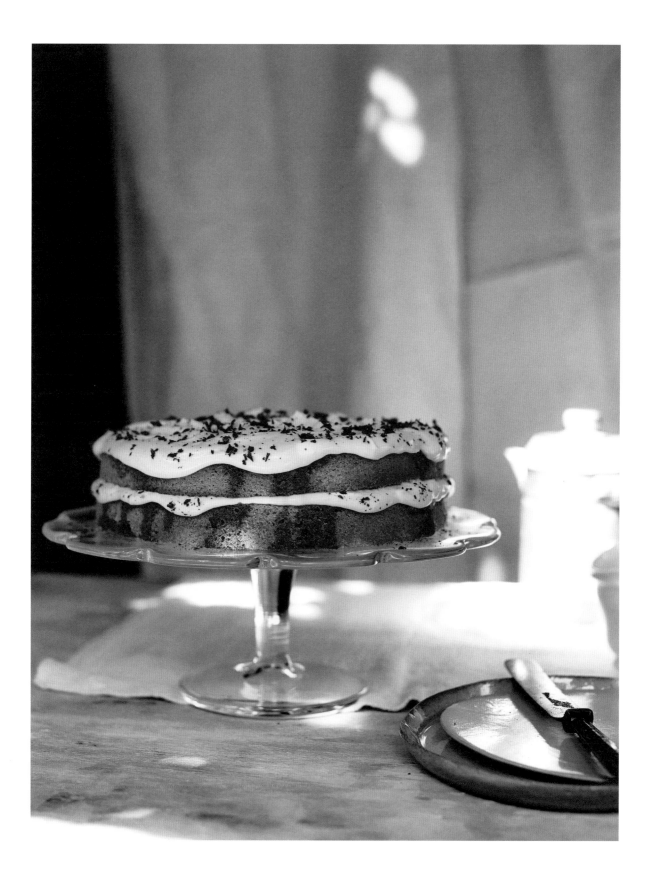

TORTA AL TIRAMISU

TIRAMISU CAKE

This is a twist on the popular Italian dessert. The sponge cake is a classic *pan di Spagna,* often the basis of most Italian celebration cakes, which is brushed with espresso coffee and filled with a creamy mascarpone filling. It can be served as an after-dinner dessert or for teatime. If you are not serving it immediately, store it in the refrigerator until required.

Cooking time: 35–40 minutes

Serves 6–8

For the *pan di Spagna* **cake:**
butter, for greasing
3 eggs
scant ½ cup/3¼ oz/90 g sugar
¾ cup/3¼ oz/90 g all-purpose flour, sifted
a pinch of table salt
1 tsp vanilla extract

For the coffee mixture:
⅔ cup/150 ml espresso coffee
1 tbsp sugar
1 tbsp Marsala wine, *Passito* (Italian straw wine), or other liqueur

For the cream:
generous 1 cup/9 oz/250 g mascarpone
3 tbsp sugar
2 egg yolks
½ cup/120 ml heavy cream
2 tbsp Marsala wine, or other liqueur

¾ oz/20 g dark or bittersweet chocolate, grated, to decorate

Preheat the oven to 350°F/180°C. Grease and line 2 × 8-in/20-cm round cake pans with parchment paper or, for extra speed, use pre-made cake pan liners.

Prepare a pot of espresso coffee, remove from the heat, and set aside.

For the cake, whisk the eggs and sugar together in a large bowl for about 5 minutes, until light and fluffy and the sugar has dissolved (to help speed up the process, add a drop of hot water). Fold in the flour, salt, and vanilla extract. Pour into the prepared pans and bake in the hot oven for 17–20 minutes. Insert a skewer into the center to test it; if it comes out clean, the cake is done. Set aside to cool a little in the pan.

Meanwhile, combine the cooled espresso coffee, sugar, and wine and set aside.

For the cream, whisk together the mascarpone, sugar, egg yolks, and heavy cream in a bowl, until light and fluffy. Fold in the wine just before assembling the cake to avoid splitting the mixture.

Remove the cakes from the pans while still warm, but cool enough to handle. Remove the parchment paper/liners and, using a pastry brush, brush the coffee mixture over both sides of the cakes. Leave to soak in for about 5 minutes. Spread one of the cakes with about half of the cream mixture and sprinkle with some of the grated chocolate, then sandwich with the top layer of cake. Spread the remaining cream over the top and sprinkle with the last of the chocolate.

TIRAMISU ALLE FRAGOLE DI ADRIANA

ADRIANA'S STRAWBERRY TIRAMISU

Light and summery, this is my sister's tiramisu recipe, which she often makes for family occasions. It's perfect for kids, as it contains no coffee (and the alcohol is optional!), but is packed with lots of healthy fruit. You can serve it immediately or make it in advance and store in the refrigerator, if you prefer.

Cooking time: 25–30 minutes (including prep)

Serves 6

2 pints/1 lb 9 oz/700 g strawberries, hulled
juice and zest of 1 lemon
1 tbsp limoncello liqueur (optional)
⅔ cup/4¾ oz/130 g superfine sugar
4 egg yolks
scant 1 cup/7 oz/200 g mascarpone
1 cup/250 ml heavy cream
10½ oz/300 g *savoiardi* cookies (soft Italian
    ladyfingers)
½ cup/3½ oz/100 g mixed berries
fresh mint (optional)

Roughly chop 1½ pints/1 lb 2 oz/500 g of the strawberries and combine with the lemon juice, limoncello (if using), and 4 tablespoons of the sugar, cover with plastic wrap, and place in the refrigerator while you prepare the creamy filling.

Whisk the egg yolks and remaining scant ½ cup/2¾ oz/80 g sugar, until light and creamy. Add the mascarpone and continue to whisk until well amalgamated and creamy. Stir in the heavy cream and mix well with a spoon. Refrigerate while you prepare the strawberry sauce.

Take the macerated strawberries out of the refrigerator and blend until smooth in a food processor or blender.

Line a deep serving dish or trifle bowl with a little of the creamy mixture. Dip the *savoiardi* cookies into the strawberry sauce and arrange them over the top of the creamy mixture. Spread more of the creamy mixture over the fingers and continue making layers like this, until you have finished all the ingredients, ending with a cream layer. Decorate the top with the remaining whole strawberries, the mixed berries, and a few sprigs of fresh mint if you have it. You can serve immediately, if you wish, or put it back in the refrigerator until you are ready.

INDEX

MY THANKS TO

Liz Przybylski for writing the recipes and chapter introductions; Adriana Contaldo for testing the recipes and cooking at the shoots; Kim Lightbody for beautiful photos; Becci Woods for lovely food styling; Alexander Breeze for selecting lovely props; Emily Preece-Morrison for editing; Stephanie Milner for all your help bringing everyone together; Laura Russell for the gorgeous design; Laura Brodie for supreme production; Komal Patel for getting the word out; Polly Powell for publishing this book and Luigi Bonomi for making it happen.

D0926849